INSIDE OUT

Stories from a Spiritual Sabbatical

DOWN UNDER

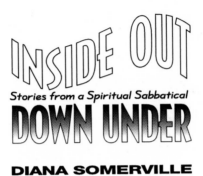

DIANA SOMERVILLE

Beechworth Press
Port Angeles, Washington

INSIDE OUT • DOWN UNDER
Stories from a Spiritual Sabbatical
by Diana Somerville

Published by Beechworth Press
P.O. Box 744, Port Angeles, Washington 98362 USA
www.beechworthpress.com

Cover art by Carmel Middletent, Clallam County, Washington
Book design and production by Ruth Marcus, Sequim, Washington

ISBN: 978-09773533-0-3

CONTENTS

PREFACE

Approaching fifty, that mid-life milestone, I overflowed with questions. How were my significant relationships changing? After years as a single mother, could I reclaim a healthy relationship with my now-grown daughters? My most recent relationship with a man had fizzled, like so many others before. Was that an omen, a sign, or simply the luck of the draw?

A women's circle had been central to my life for nearly twenty years, providing spiritual nourishment and emotional learning, but I had trouble seeing the group continuing into the indefinite future. What did that mean? My work as a freelance writer, editor, and occasional teacher was fine, if not dazzling. Could I create something more dynamic, more vital?

Beyond the personal loomed even larger concerns: As a feminist, I wondered about the future in a culture that devalues so much of the feminine and fears the very process of aging. Raised as an environmentalist, I was increasingly concerned about humanity's relationship with Earth and all its inhabitants. It seemed like every day working as a science writer I saw more evidence of imbalance in those connections.

I knew it was time to reconnect with my authentic self, wherever she might be. My spirit longed to embrace the deep wisdom of the natural world, while some unnamed part of myself wondered how best to live on an increasingly beleaguered planet. The women who surrounded me urged me to follow my dreams.

So I did what many people long to: I took a leave of absence from my everyday existence, left my longtime home in Boulder, Colorado, and went to live an upside-down year in a small rural Australian town where my brother had settled years before.

Wombats and warbling magpies, flower-strewn desert tracks, and ancient rocks taught me to to listen in new ways and seek my own song lines. The intricate spiritual connections between Australian Aborigines and Earth's oldest continent offered some surprisingly powerful teachings. The Aborigines' ancient ways contrasted sharply with the rugged individualism valued in the American West, while evoking echoes of Native American cultures.

My spiritual sabbatical embraced family and friends, journeys in dreams and while awake, as well as Australia's people and landscapes. And though I went looking for answers, I gradually found myself embracing much larger mysteries.

I offer the story of my journey with the hope that some of it may touch your heart as it did mine. While some names and details in this story have been changed to protect people's privacy, I've stayed true to the essence of each experience.

ACKNOWLEDGMENTS

So many women have given me love and laughter and encouragement, strength, courage, and wisdom that I can hardly name them all. By holding up a truthful mirror, providing a moral compass, and a constant source of amazement, they continue to teach me and touch my heart, inspire and renew me. They fill me with hope that the divine feminine is vibrantly alive and transforming the world as it reawakens the divine feminine within all of us, regardless of gender.

I owe unending gratitude to the vibrant women who have encircled me, one way or another: Alana, Alice, Barbara, Debbie, Doris, Eve, Frances, Jean, Jennifer, Joyce, Kris, Nancy, Pat, Peggy, Ronnie, Sue, Vickie, and Yvonne. I trust they will continue to be woven into the fabric of my life. Special thanks are due to my mother and grandmothers, my daughters and granddaughters, my sisters and nieces, for their ongoing lessons; to my brother, for constantly renewing my appreciation for the world's special men, and to my grandson for offering hope for a future filled with more wonderful men. You are all my teachers.

Thanks also to my writing group, to Marilyn and Ruth, for inspiration in birthing this book, and to Carmel for carrying a living spark of Australia to Washington.

CALLED BY THE VOICE OF THE EARTH

Exposed to the power of the elements for so long, Australia's desert face is scoured clean, scraped to bedrock bones. The heart of Earth's oldest continent is the Red Centre, an immense desert too vast and powerful to be contemplated as a whole. White settlers named the desert bit by bit: the Tanami, the Tirari, the Strzelecki, the Simpson, the Sturt Stony Desert. One is rimmed with crimson flowers that cry like hearts turned inside out; another crusted with diamonds of salt. Some are paved with desert varnish—rocks burnished shiny red-brown as if shined with oxblood shoe polish. Some undulate with orange dunes; others are raw maroon rocks flicked with mere skiffs of sand. Each name has its own story, each desert its own character. All the deserts glint with a promise of clarity. Through the eastern quadrant of the continental basin, maps show the vein-like lacework of the ghostly Dimatina River, a netting of sandy rivulets and dusty watercourses that lies empty of water for years on end, open in aching anticipation.

"Camel handlers from Afghanistan were the first non-natives able to cope with these deserts," said my newly acquired friend Robin as we sat outside our musty-smelling canvas tent. The desert sun dropped slowly, its softening light transforming nearly colorless sand dunes into dreamy ocean waves.

According to the sketchy maps we'd been given, Robin and I were somewhere near a tiny settlement called Maree along the Birdsville Track, the remnants of an old camel route that skimmed the edge of Australia's great artesian basin. We were heading for Alice Springs, tracing, on the ground, the route flown by Australia's legendary Royal Flying Doctor Service. Its small planes are still the only practical way to provide medical care to people scattered over more than five thousand miles of desert.

"Naturally, the Afghanis brought their camel saddles from home, and whatever stuffing they used to pad saddles a century ago happened to contain the seeds of rosy dock," she continued, waving toward the improbable purple flowers fringing the roadside, her dark eyes gleaming as she warmed to the tale. "Hard desert riding loosened the saddle stuffing bit by bit so that now, whenever spring brings a trace of rain, the old camel tracks erupt with an extravagance of pink and purple blooms," she said, her gentle British accent incising each detail with assurance. Robin, I was learning, easily dipped into decades of stories gathered while living in Denmark, Peru, and now Australia.

The accidental blossoms of rosy dock, as hearty as the cameleers who spread them, seemed both a jubilant relic and a promise of renewal for those like me who came to Australia to track their dreams. Feeling an odd kinship with long-gone camel traders crisscrossing these alien deserts, I wondered what stray bits might escape from my own baggage, what serpentine trail my own remnants might trace.

The path that brought me to Australia emerged from listening to my own dreams, awakening each morning to record what wisps I could. Some glimmering, elusive dreaming had led me here, to seek the clarity of desert starkness; I marveled that after months of dreams, at last I sat, opening myself to the glinting, knife-edge beauty of salt crystal springs. The red sand and orange dust hummed with dreams. I strained to hear their muffled harmonies as a wordless excitement sang through every cell of my body, alive to the haunting magic of this place.

Evening stillness enveloped our tent, pitched where scallops of salt marked the ghostly edges of the phantom Lake Eyre; unfamiliar stars danced above the desert dreamscape, cloaking us with enduring comfort, drawing us close within their stately tapestry of change.

A highlight of our trek would be a visit to that icon of the Australian outback, Ayers Rock, an immense stranded inland dune turned to stone, standing more than a thousand feet above a scalded inland sandscape. Its real name is Uluru, say the Anangu people, those to whom the land belongs, those who keep its stories. I longed to learn the meaning of this name.

Layers of names, meanings, stories, and dreamings overlay the entire Australian continent, home of Earth's most ancient rocks. For thousands of years—some say twenty thousand, some say more than two hundred thousand—only its native people entwined their legends, language, and spiritual practices with this land, the only culture to remain so long undisturbed by outside invaders. Over millennia, they have trod every bit of their piece of the earth, absorbing its lessons through their bodies, listening to its stories, breathing in every inch of the landscape. Perhaps the earth speaks so powerfully in Australia because its people have sung it all into responsiveness and learned to listen to its answers, to dance its rhythms, and sing its songs.

But I'm getting ahead of myself, moving beyond the familiar chronological pattern. Once the line between past and present dissolves, keeping track of time gradually seems pointless. Somehow Australia, the land beyond time, the place time forgot, had already melted away the need for sequence even before I thought about leaving Colorado.

Part of my journey began in Boulder, when I first heard someone play a didgeridoo, that primitive, uniquely Australian instrument, which awakened my yearning for new ways to listen.

An odd chance drew me to that sound in an unlikely ad hoc art gallery that had taken shape in a scrabbly warehouse district on the north edge of Boulder. My friend Alice mentioned hearing about an exhibit of Australian women's paintings—which flared up our shared passion for experiencing all kinds of women's creative work. At home in both Mexico, where she grew up, and the States, where she'd lived much of her adult life, Alice was beautifully bi-cultural and blessed with an uncanny instinct for sniffing out intriguing expressions of women's culture from around the world. Over the years, as we'd watched our colt-legged daughters grow into dizzying young women, Alice and I watched incomprehensible Japanese films, took in vibrant Hmong needlework, bounced and clapped our way through African dance performance and sought out countless exotic art exhibitions. So it was almost second nature for us to take on this hunt, venturing into a small industrial district we'd never seen before, though we'd lived in Boulder for decades. Next to a plumbing supply store, behind a machine shop that overhauled engines, we glimpsed a cinder-block building with a hand-lettered sign: "Aboriginal Women's Art."

Drawing closer, we heard an insistent, hypnotic drone, interwoven with startling howls and eerie, bird-like chirps. We entered the space, following the sounds to a corner where we saw a middle-aged man, red faced, round and bearded, his cheeks puffed out like bellows, blowing into a wooden tube nearly as long as he was tall. We waited as the haunting harmonic reverberations slowly dissolved.

"What is that?" we asked, almost in unison.

"A didgeridoo. In Australia, it's played for fun—as well as for special rituals," he replied, delighted at being caught playing. A Boulder musician recently returned from down under, Jim happily related how the Aborigines befriended him, once they realized he appreciated their music.

The gallery walls hummed with the energy of the paintings: circle after circle of dots radiating out from center points. Flecks of gold, brown, ochre, red, a breath of white, an occasional flash of green transformed the room into a multi-dimensional echo chamber. Segmented worms, shields, sticks, and horseshoe shapes danced in vivid but somber hues, touching something primal in me. The images on the walls resonated with the same insistent, pulsing rhythm that Jim's breath brought from the didgeridoo. I urged him to tell us whatever he could about the paintings, the instruments, the music.

"While the dizzying patterns of Australian Aboriginal art may look abstract to our eyes, they're not abstractions at all," Jim said. "They're actually landscapes that show Earth as seen from above." In the European landscape tradition, a bird's-eye view is an alien perspective. But for those who directly experience the earth through the soles of their feet, it's a natural point of view.

The artists had patiently mimicked the movement of song lines, using dots to outline the shapes of the women's dreamings: the wild onion dreaming, the witchiti grub dreaming. Alien yet hauntingly familiar, like the branching of neurons that know no up or down, no dark or light, the patterns of the women's sacred stories whispered of hidden gates to other worlds. Doorways to Earth-knowing, they traced the Mysterious underlying beneath the familiar, like an eerie glimpse of bones beneath a much-loved face.

Streams of tiny dots mapped the waves of energy for eyes accustomed to seeing only in the wavelengths of visible light. Shimmering, repetitive lines of paint traced the energy patterns of water holes or invisible, underground rivers.

Evoking maps of shamans' journeys from some long-forgotten book or the sinuous spell of Mexican Huichol yarn paintings, the women's canvases conjured countless haunting images, awakening me to powerful, half-remembered dreams. Dreams of healing energies; journeys that awakened new possibilities; walls that dissolved into patterns of light; objects that danced into life singing stories with profound, indecipherable meanings.

"What connects the images and the sounds of the didgeridoo?" I asked.

"A traditional didgeridoo is a tree hollowed out naturally by insects," Jim said, eagerly responding to my interest. "Eating their way along, they create a whole labyrinth of tunnels, a unique pattern of sounding chambers. Someone picks it up in the bush—not quite sure how that works—and then it's decorated for a ceremony, painted with colored ocher and clay, in traditional patterns just like these paintings," he said, waving his arms to encompass the whole gallery.

"But the sounds?" I asked, spellbound.

"They're songs and stories. As people gathered around the campfire, someone would play the didgeridoo, releasing the song, breathing its story to life."

"You mean there's a separate didgeridoo for each story?"

"The didgeridoo is the voice of that tree branch, those ants, that exact spot on the earth," he said. "Or maybe it's the other way around: The voice is already in the branch, just waiting for someone to come along and recognize it. When the ritual or corroboree ended, the didgeridoo would be returned to the bush and placed exactly where it was found, to keep its story until it needed to be sung and heard again."

I couldn't help laughing. "So the bush is full of elaborately decorated didgeridoos, just lying around?"

He smiled at the image. "Well, traditionally, that's what they did," he said, caressing the instrument he held. "The didgeridoo plays a special role, helping preserve their culture. Just imagine the scene—painted bodies flashing in the dark around a fire-lit circle. Droning chants, the rhythm of sticks clacking together, the haunting wail of the didgeridoo, they all create a sort of trance-like state. I think it explains how their culture survives with no written language. How else could they memorize all the stories?"

"Interesting. You mean that tribal people knew the power of hypnotic suggestion?"

"Maybe they wouldn't say it that way," he hesitated, "but somehow the elders knew that sound and rhythm plant information in a non-verbal part of the brain."

"And our brain researchers are only now exploring other kinds of remembering," I marveled, recalling some article I'd read.

Alice walked toward more than a dozen instruments leaning against the gallery wall and asked, "Are all these traditional didgeridoos?"

"Well, the designs are traditional, but they're not sacred objects, if that's what you mean. They were made for me to bring back. Nowadays, lots of didjs are made for the tourist trade. Didjs are becoming so popular, I've even seen 'em made out of PVC pipe. But these were made by traditional people."

Having mastered the circular breathing pattern that coaxed sounds from the didgeridoo, Jim returned to Boulder with unexpected treasures. "I'm still not quite sure why I brought more than a hundred Aboriginal women's paintings, besides the didgeridoos and click sticks," he said, chuckling and shaking his head in wonder. "I went to Australia to learn to play the didgeridoo and returned as a sort of inadvertent art dealer."

Embarking with one purpose and finding another along the way struck a subtle chord within me. I realized that I was on a bit of a quest myself as I approached my fiftieth year. I knew that year represented a hinge point in a woman's life, one that needed a special kind of marking. I was looking for a way to explore my own spiritual path, just as other women had taken African safaris, Indian pilgrimages, or treks to Tibet, but none of those places called to me.

In Boulder, a kaleidoscope of women provided my enduring emotional base and my spiritual center. They were full of creative ideas, and I listened to how they devised their own celebrations with apparent ease. I joined Jennifer for a regal dinner party she threw for herself, to honor her becoming queen of her own destiny and danced with Peggy at her sock-hop where we all became teenagers for the night. Susan tattooed her ankle with the footprint of a wolf, symbolizing her permanent commitment to preserving wilderness. Kris bicycled the Continental Divide. Physical challenges were popular: running a marathon, taking up skydiving, or "bagging a fourteener"—climbing one of Colorado's fourteen-thousand-foot peaks.

But no one else's dream seemed to fit the paradox I found myself wrestling with: I longed for meaningful changes even though my life didn't require a complete overhaul. I felt myself moving from patterns that centered on relationships with men and concern for my daughters toward something larger and less well defined. But without a clear goal, I wondered how could I shake loose the sticky bits, invite in some gentle transformation, without unleashing wholesale destruction.

Neither work nor relationships bound me to Boulder. Divorced for nearly twenty years, I had raised my two daughters on my own and, over the years, created a comfy niche as a modestly successful freelance science writer. Colorado's researchers usually offered enough work to keep me afloat and Boulder, a college town, provided a yeasty mix of cultural zip and mountain grandeur. As my half-century mark approached, my daughters, Catlyn and Kerry, grown up and living on their own, no longer needed major mothering.

In a dream, I saw a woman, relaxed and calm, sitting in a lotus position submerged beneath the surface of a pool. While chaos reigned above, she floated in tranquility, eyes closed, smiling softly—a symbol of an unknown part of my self waiting to surface. The woman meditating underwater was the first of many dreams that helped me realize that I needed to take a few steps off my well-trod daily path. My moderately bold and slightly loopy goal became clearer: I'd take a leave of absence, spend my whole fiftieth year living differently.

Then practical questions appeared like bubbles rising to the surface. Where to go? What to do? And how could I afford to live a year without working?

Where to go? Australia instantly came to mind—not only because it is the land of the Dreaming. I began amassing reasons, starting with my brother, who had left for Australia more than fifteen years before and settled in a little town called Beechworth in northeast Victoria. Although our contacts were warm, they'd been infrequent—which didn't keep me from still missing him. His occasional letters said that his comfy, small-town life didn't make for newsy dispatches; he and his wife, both in their second marriages, were almost boringly happy.

Boring happiness seemed a paradox worth exploring.

In contrast to his contentment, I found relationships with men came and went in my life, often shifting as abruptly as Colorado's mile-high weather. My most recent one, a tumultuous two years with Matt, had met a sudden, unforeseen end that left me wounded and wondering, again, about the significance of yet another man promising partnership and then walking away.

No doubt, my soul, my psyche needed some velvet time to reflect, to renew and replenish on deeper levels. Was there a way to change that tediously familiar pattern with men? Did I even need to? Where did men fit in the next big chapter of my life?

Living abroad, without the stress of another language or the challenges of adjusting to a radically different culture, would gently turn everything upside down and free me for quiet contemplation. Seasons in the southern hemisphere were reversed, the skies splashed with unfamiliar constellations. Earth's oldest continent is mostly an enormous desert that had once been ocean floor—the geological opposite of the relatively youthful Colorado Rockies. A year down under would shift my world softly like drifting flakes settling in a snow globe.

If only I could sort out the money problem. Looking for a job in Australia wasn't an option, given the immigration laws, while continuing to scramble for freelance assignments would mean changing only the scenery, not the substance, of my day-to-day world.

Although it was expensive to be a tourist in Australia, living in little country towns was affordable, said my brother, Quinn. "If you wouldn't mind trading the sleepy pace of

Beechworth for the bustle of Boulder, I'll bet I can find some nice little flat for you to rent."

Could I figure out how to afford to live without working? The idea seemed daring, but maybe not impossible. Mulling my options one evening with my friend Debbie, she suddenly lit up: "Your house is more than a monthly bill to be paid— it's also an asset," she said. "Can't you rent it for more than your mortgage payment?" There was always a demand for rentals in Boulder. Our back-of-the-envelope calculations showed that, with a suitable tenant and a year's lease, I could do it.

And so I came to Australia, the place we call the Land Down Under, much the way Africa is the Dark Continent; maps and globes depict the world of the white man on top, above—an orientation that's more than a mapmaking convention or a simple cartographic convenience. What's above is superior, exalted, dominant, in control, in the light. Down under is beneath one's feet, beneath notice, insignificant, hidden. Below is mysterious and menacing. One falls down, is pulled below, is trapped underneath. Descending is not a journey taken willingly. What does it mean to be in the dark?

Above, the sun god—call him Apollo, call him Ra—still rules over the rational and reasonable, the realm of the daylight, waking world. Down under, cloaked in darkness, lies the mysterious land of dreaming—a division as clear as day and night.

The gradations between light and dark begin to hint and murmur, as twilight softens contrasts, blurring the boundaries between thought and feelings. The sun sets and the sky dissolves, gradually revealing the night sky vastness, first one star, then another. Dazzled by daylight's Apollonian brilliance, we lose track of the immensity of our universe, forget what only the dark can reveal. Light can conceal, keeping us from remembering that the stars are always out, always there, whether we see them or not. The sky brings a nightly reminder of what Jung and Freud tried to tell us—and something tribal people have always known: our waking consciousness, what we see in the daylight, shapes our view of the world.

What can be seen only when there is no light? And what calls me, connects me to that unseen world of the sky-schooled, of the people of the Dreaming, who learn from night's overarching darkness? Tribal people know every visible landscape is overlaid with meaning, just as an apparently dry riverbed can conceal a bush banquet. The broad sandstone cathedrals define the sacred; each rocky outcropping tells a story.

After years spent in women's circles, doing our female version of Jungian dream work, I'd grown to trust the dark, not fear it. Pulling away layer after layer of meaning in our dreams thrilled me as the swirling images revealed the personal and the primal. Venturing down under, to the land of the Dreaming, tugged at the edges of my awareness, expanding the way learning a new word suddenly makes it appear everywhere.

Hopelessly, passionately curious, I can't help pursuing countless topics that intrigue me, and probing for new meanings, weaving seemingly improbable links between the ideas I encounter and my own experiences. I keep seeking the bigger patterns that resonate with meaning. This quirk is both a blessing and a curse as a science writer. I love learning for its own sake, but it's a real nuisance not knowing when to stop researching, gathering information, looking for patterns, and spotting interconnections. Sometimes I attribute all this to being a double Gemini who, by her very nature, sees at least four aspects to everything.

Every aspect of spending time in Australia, of exploring the rich interweaving of people and place, land and dreaming, made me tingle with a special kind of excitement. I suspect it's what theologians now call "holy envy." The people were one with the landscape in a deeper way than Western culture allowed.

For instance, I heard of one story that came from some time in the mid-1980s when the Australian government convened a council of elders from across the desert to help in the ongoing process of settling land claims. One by one, the city dwellers came before the council and were asked to do the dance of their place and sing its song so the elders could see the strength and clarity of their connections. When one began to express his claim, the elders shook their heads. "No, No. Not this land. Two hundred kilometers west," they declared. So familiar with the link between people and land, story and place, the elders knew every song of the disputed desert by heart.

My own heritage seemed bleak by comparison.

Child of an empire where the sun never sets, my legacy was too much contrast and not enough shadows. No songs, no dances, my heritage traced back to Roger Williams, the man who founded Rhode Island as an oasis of spiritual freedom. My nine-times great-grandfather believed that the only honorable way to acquire land from the Narragansett Indians was to buy it—another idea too radical for his time. Today, I have none of the stories from his life, know of no songs he sang his children, only a small, scallop-edged plate with pink flowers, a crack through its center glued together. This odd little artifact has been handed down through the years while the generations lost their way, embracing newness as a guide, creating a New World with too many dazzling pieces and too few enduring patterns.

I recalled the vibrant unsettling energy of the Australian women's paintings as I drifted on the energetic currents flowing between past and present, ancient and modern. The patterns portrayed the energy the women experienced emanating from the earth as they neared an underground water source or a patch of wild yams growing, timeless harmonies of the Dreaming, as Jim, the guardian of the exhibit, explained. The women had experienced those signature patterns since the beginning of time, but until a missionary showed them how to use paint and canvas, they'd never tried to portray the subtle earth messages they felt.

Perhaps not so odd, I thought, that Jim had hauled back nearly a hundred large canvases and mounted an exhibition of Aboriginal paintings when all he had intended was simply learning to play the didgeridoo. The musician returned with far more than sounds and songs and instruments. When Alice and I stumbled on the exhibition, I had no idea about the connections between the earth, the dancing dots of earth energy, and the deep vibrations of the didgeridoo, nor any notion that they would work their magic on me, too.

I found myself drawn by the compelling sounds from Australia's heart and the women's rhythmic, dancing images to a place where dreams join the waking world, with experiences beyond all my cultural reference points. Once I'd emerged from my own journey down under, I began to see different connections joined like a spider web. Each web fits a unique dimension of space; the shape formed by this tree branch, that weed stem, and this rock is singular. Yet every spider carries a genetic sense of pattern so strong that each species can be identified by its own weaving characteristics. A web is at once incredibly particular—a transitory, ephemeral net to trap the chance insect passing by—and timelessly shaped by instinctual gifts as old as arachnids themselves. So delicate that it is easily swept aside with the wave of the hand, spider silk weaves connections so strong, flexible, and sensitive that every touch reverberates throughout the web. Spider silk heals; spider webs can staunch the flow of blood.

The women of my circles—Alice and Jean, Doris and Peggy, Yvonne, Joyce and Kris—have become my trees; Alana, Deborah, Sue, and Jennifer are my rocks, as I weave the web of my own inner knowing and explore what connects me to them, to my deepest self, through our meetings, rituals, and deep sharing. I longed for the chance to reflect on this web and explore the meaning behind its primal patterns.

At the same time, another part of the web connects me to my brother, Quinn, who left Boulder to live in Australia nearly two decades before. I followed him down under. What remained of our earlier connections, wisped together by too-infrequent letters and even rarer phone calls? I trusted that the process of living the dream, writing, and remembering would gradually reveal other web-like connections. Following the turns and curves of thought patterns, exploring all the conjunctions, serendipitous and unlikely, revealed patterns that transcend the continents and leap across time.

WOMBAT WELCOME

Initially, I got to Australia by conventional means. As the pilot announced our approach to Melbourne, I struggled with airsickness and a migraine headache fed by the aircraft air full of perfume, overcooked coffee, and the concentrated food and body odors of a day-long flight. Then suddenly the flight attendants marched down the aisle and, in a surprising but obviously familiar drill, threw open every closet and overhead compartment, spraying insecticide into every cranny with practiced ferocity. A disembodied voice intoned mechanical assurances that the spray was harmless, an almost quaint Australian precaution, as the toxic fog thickened. When the plane's doors finally opened, I lurched off, pale and clammy, abandoning any fantasies of symbolic beginnings and meaningful experiences for a breath of fresh air.

Queasy, I cooled my head on a chrome-plated luggage cart, wondering how Quinn had changed, then glimpsed him waving excitedly just beyond the customs officials. Now with streaks of silver highlighting his beard, he wore the same Greek fisherman's hat he'd worn when he left Boulder. With one warm and loving hug, he swept away any uncertainty. Gradually sinking into the softening bitumen surface of the car park, we stood smiling, staring at each other with goofy disbelief.

"Is that the same hat?" I asked, forcing my voice past the lump of joyful tears in my throat.

"Well, sure, it's the same hat—though I've replaced it a few times," he said with a grin, "sort of like the fellow who's had the same hammer thirty years, though he's replaced the handle four times and the head twice."

"But he's wearing the shoes he brought from America. They must be twenty-five years old," his new wife, Tia, added with a chuckle.

"Not much call for wearing fancy shoes in Beechworth, so I sure haven't worn them out," he said, dancing a quick jig step.

The Australian twang in his voice was different but the air of cheerful stewardship was exactly the same. I could almost hear our grandmother declaring, "Use it up or wear it out, make it do or do without." Quinn and I had adopted her adage as a guiding principle, much to the amusement of our sister, Isabel. Somehow shoes and clothes, curtains and chairs were to be discarded and replaced according to a timetable known only to the sibling born between us, not to me or Quinn.

"I got these at Phantasmagoria, that leather shop on University Hill. Is it still there? They were the best leather crafters I'd ever seen," he said, his admiration for their skill still fresh.

"It's clear they were made to last," said Tia, brown eyes crinkled with amusement, her words echoing grandma without ever having known her. Instantly, I knew that Tia cherished the traits that our sister, Isabel, scorned, transforming husbandry into stinginess with her ever-so-slightly derisive laugh. Tia was an ally, one who knew the basic rightness of living lightly, getting by and enjoying it. I gulped in a big breath of relief, releasing a worry about meeting the woman Quinn had met and married since I'd last seen him. Not much of a letter writer, he had given me only the sketchiest details about his divorce—or even why he and his first wife had first decided to immigrate to her native Australia.

That day, I realized how much I'd longed for a sister with Tia's qualities—including her somehow intuiting the importance of introducing me to the secret charms of wombats straight away. Tying my luggage in the back of their pickup truck, they proclaimed the first stop on the way to the tiny town of Beechworth was Healesville for an essential part of my visit. "Have you ever seen a wombat?" Tia asked. I had to admit that, even though its name evoked a familiar chuckle, I had only the haziest notion of what a wombat looked like.

"No trip to Oz is complete without being properly introduced to the elusive koala and the under-appreciated wombat," Quinn declared with mock solemnity as we pulled into the gravel in front of the wildlife sanctuary.

Wildlife is an ironically unsuitable term, I soon learned. Because of the often searing daytime heat, most Australian critters are shy, reserved creatures of the night that doze through daylight hours.

Staring into the shadows of the granite rocks outside its burrow, I couldn't distinguish the snoozing, brownish-gray wombat until Tia pointed it out. Less than two feet high with short legs, a thick body and almost no tail, a wombat is often nearly as wide as tall. Its rounded ears, small eyes, and a naked, leathery nose gave it the look of a slightly bemused teddy bear.

The wombat stared at me for a moment, asking to be known beyond its whimsical name, to have its paradoxical nature be understood.

"In the bush, it's not unusual to encounter a wombat slowly ambling along a back road, and if car and wombat collide, it's usually the wombat who picks itself up, shakes off the dust, and continues on its way, unconcerned with the damaged vehicle or its shaken driver," Tia said. "They're as sturdy as a boulder."

Close to the ground, a wombat feels the pulse of the earth, listens to its vibrations, and moves with contemplative slowness. It grazes thoughtfully, snuffling along, nose to the ground, occasionally scruffing loose a tender morsel or uprooting an especially delicious grassy nibble with long, sturdy front claws designed for digging. Although naturally shy or perhaps solitary, the wombat is not easily frightened—an important distinction. It doesn't flee but stands its ground.

The more I learned, the more I found myself drawn to these creatures—perhaps because when they're feeling uncertain or threatened, wombats' first response is to dig, dig, dig. To go underground. To get below the surface. And what of the name, wombat? The dictionary calls it a native word, but my imagination transformed it into a bat of the womb, another creature comfortable upside down in the dark.

With Earth's down-under rhythms, Nature has created a tranquil symphony of evolutionary variations on the theme of marsupials. Wombats and possums, koalas and kangaroos, the most familiar, hint at their clever diversity. Tiny mulgara, dibblers and marsupial mice, bandicoots and wallabies are just a few of the creatures who share an astonishing, unlikely reproductive strategy.

To me, there was something deeply touching about the way marsupial mothers give birth to potential; the tiny, vulnerable embryo needs the deep nurturing of its mother's pouch. Thimble-sized, a wombat embryo leaves the birth canal hairless, its eyes welded shut, and instantly it tests—or perhaps reaffirms—the safety of its world with the initiation rite: Crawling and tugging through a forest of coarse fur, blind and helpless, it must find its own way to its mother's second womb. Once safely within the pouch a nipple awaits and there it holds on for dear life, taking in nourishment, slowly growing large enough to peer out of mother's pouch.

"'Pouch' is the wrong word," Jilba said when I met her months later, as she let me cuddle the baby wombat that had been orphaned near her farm. "A pouch is like a pocket, loose and floppy, but a marsupial pouch is muscular, tight, and vagina-like. The marsupial embrace is so snug that a kangaroo can bound across the desert at more than thirty miles an hour and still keep her little joey safe."

That must mean that, deep within their DNA, embedded in each marsupial's evolutionary bones, is a profound sense of trust, I mused. Its legacy is a safe world; Australia a land of few predators. There are poisonous but usually reclusive snakes. The Tasmanian devil, an extraordinary carnivorous marsupial, had once been scarce and is now extinct on mainland Australia. Later I learned that tribal elders kept the predators in balance as part of their responsibilities.

Time had brought changes to the marsupial's Eden, Quinn and Tia explained, taking turns introducing me to the bush landscape as we drove to Beechworth. The dog-like wild dingo was introduced by people sailing over from the Pacific Islands. Then came the white men, bringing the first hoofed creatures—cows, horses, and sheep. Foxes and rabbits, cats, and dogs, all part of the mob of squabbling predators introduced from the white man's world, now seriously threaten many native birds and smaller marsupials. As Quinn and Tia fed my yearning to know more about the interweaving of this land and its inhabitants, they also conveyed their own love of the land and their deep connection to all its idiosyncratic glories.

■ ■ ■

Becoming a science writer gave me lots of practice delving into a completely unfamiliar topic, following my nose, trying to figure out whether or not it was interesting enough to write about. Over time, I'd developed a habit of zipping through written material, then finding some knowledgeable people to talk with, but reading the modest offerings of the Beechworth library only left me hungry for more vibrant information about Australia's original inhabitants, the people of the didgeridoo, the artists who painted the earth's energy fields. Developing my own course of study, I managed to suss out a living text: Joel, who offered classes and led small groups to the area's caves and remaining rock paintings. With a Koori mother and a father who was half black and half Native American, Joel, as brown and round as a coconut, seemed genetically destined to be a cultural anthropologist. He reveled in speaking to people like me who wanted to see the plants and animals, the rivers and trees with new—or far more ancient—eyes. Building bridges between indigenous native cultures and the white people's world was a Karmic assignment he assumed with relish and good humor.

Like an eager bower bird brightening its nest with flowers and found trinkets, I wove each new splash of insight into my timeless dreamtime journey. The primal power of naming claimed a special place. For example, many people now feel "Aborigine" is demeaning, a term that recalls two hundred years of repression and near extermination. When Europeans first arrived in Australia, they called the native people "Aborigines" and spread that name around the world, laying their claim to superiority with their language; by renaming them, they blurred the people's own identities, much the way Americans renamed the indigenous American people "Indians." "Koori" is the name favored by those working for civil rights and political unity among tribes. It's a new word even for some Australians, and one I try to remember to use. It's a small acknowledgment of the gravity of what white men have done to these people who, for millennia, lived in mindful balance with their own special place on Earth.

Joel, however, spoke most often of "the people."

Those who share a totem animal are closest kin, Joel explained. All wallaby people are related to each other, all parrot people, all emu people. They know their animals' stories, songs, and rituals; know when they breed, where they live, how they thrive. The next circle of connection includes those that share the same kind of skin—fur or feathers or scales. Those with the same kind of skin are closer than cousins, more like siblings, he says. Skin sisters, skin brothers.

Skin sister. I love having a word to describe those mysteriously intimate connections that, until now, had no name. Wombats—a love for them, an affinity for their ways, a tacit understanding of wombatness—weaves into my bonds with Tia and the other skin sisters I encountered down under.

As Joel explained the next level after skin connections, I got lost in a thicket of unfamiliar detail more dense than my spider web connections. Not an uncommon response, he said. Koori kinship networks are the most intricate on Earth, so complex that anthropologists outside the web cannot follow them. Rather than try to explain the levels of connection, Koori people often take a linguistic shortcut and refer to their aunts, uncles, or cousins when talking to outsiders—who are often startled at the very idea that Koori people have close relatives everywhere on the continent, he said. These strong, subtle, multi-level ties ensure that whereever you travel on the vast Australian continent, you remain connected. Someone will always be there to welcome you and take you in.

A shared legacy—cultural, linguistic, spiritual—provided the connection. But I also hoped to find out about others, like me, who'd arrived on this island continent by choice or happenstance.

KANGAROOS AT THE THRESHOLD

The year before my journey, Barbara, a longtime friend and wellspring of outlandish images, had accurately diagnosed my symptomatic restlessness: "You've enrolled in The Tiddlywinks School of Personal Evolution," she said. "You just sit in one place for so long, like a tiddlywink. Gradually, more and more pressure is applied until finally, one day—boing! You're catapulted up into the air and don't know just where you'll land."

Once enrolled herself, she'd wound up in Cleveland.

For me, it was Beechworth, a spot so tiny that most maps omit it, so far off the beaten path that not many Australians have heard of it, a little town of less than four thousand souls, including my brother, Quinn, who has called this spot home for more than fifteen years. Could he find me a pleasant place to stay for a year? I asked, and in no time at all, he responded: A furnished flat near his workshop would be ready in January and the welcome mat was already out. How soon could I fly down?

My spacious old house in Boulder had closets under the eaves, cabinets built into chimney nooks—a dangerous amount of storage space for one person, especially one who'd rather stash than sort things any day. Without realizing it, I'd created a shrine to inertia. Packing up the home where I'd lived for nearly two decades churned up artifacts, memories, and dust. Closets overflowed with clothes that should have been given to charity and filing cabinets bulged with outdated information on topics I'd researched and written about ages ago. The attic was crammed with my daughters' relics—Kerry's kindergarten drawings, the scrapbooks Catlyn had spent her junior high years filling with photos of teen idols—and crates of papers churned up by the process of a protracted divorce. Catlyn, soon to be twenty-nine, was not yet eight when I began the messy and painful breakup with Todd. Kerry, four years younger, would be twenty-five. I had no idea if these teddy bear time capsules held any memories my grown girls might cherish.

Decades of delayed decisions crept out of the crannies, demanding to be addressed. Clearing out the physical and emotional cobwebs provided a fitting prelude to a less busy, more introspective time—and confirmed my slightly mad notion to tiddlywink out of my well-worn patterns. Friends "adopted" furniture for the duration, storing my computer and boxes of books and dishes. Even with their help, it took weeks to whittle down the wreckage to the ninety pounds the airline allowed for my odyssey, to find a woman willing to rent my house and caretake my two aging, set-in-their-ways cats.

Once the departure date was final, my women's circle gathered for a farewell ritual. One by one, each woman gave me a wish to carry on my journey, each symbolized by tiny objects we called talis-women: a moonstone, a bead that evoked the earth as seen from space, a spiral of silver, a beautiful button, "because often it's the small, simple things that help us keep things together," Nancy said with characteristic insight. Joyce, the expert craftswoman, had fashioned a tiny fringed bag, not three inches across, of velvety purple leather. The shells, beads, and feathers adorning it represented the four directions, she explained. Placing the medicine bag around my neck, she said, "Remember, you are taking this journey for all of us." I cried.

Most of our rituals ended with an uproarious feast. This time, the feast provided an antidote to my tears.

"You have to guess the theme of the food," Alice said, placing a bowl of guacamole beside a basket of blue corn chips.

"Tofu enchiladas!" said Doris, who always favored soy instead of dairy. "Now she'll know for sure."

"Boulder food!" I exclaimed. Peals of laughter followed as Nancy and Peg, Kris and Joyce, Yvonne and Jean each explained in hilarious detail why the particular treat she had decided to bring would not be easy to come by in Australia.

Their good wishes, their excitement at my boldness, their enthusiasm for my fill-in-the-blank venture, and our shared tears and laughter splashed over me.

Our weekly gatherings had provided my emotional center for more years than I'd been married; our connections, celebrations, and rituals were the warp and weft with which I'd woven the fabric of my life. Joining hands in a circle to contemplate the significance of events in our lives often provided my only moments of quiet introspection—and a regular source of laughter. Lighting candles to honor the elemental forces of earth, air, fire, and water, the four directions and the shift of the seasons were part of the quiet rituals that reconnected us with The Continuous Woman—the larger shape of our lives.

While the connections around the circle were far too vibrant for me to take for granted, by some odd little mental hiccup, I hadn't realized that a year away meant a year not shared with them. That final evening of farewells opened the doorway to another new experience—a full cycle of seasons without the circle.

"I can't imagine going more than a week without looking at all your dear faces," I said, with an odd sinking feeling, as if I'd been condemned to live for a year without ever being able to look into a mirror.

"You'll see us, all right," said Kris. "I'll make sure of it." We often joked about how Kris's camera was part of what made our rituals sacred, but that fat packet of photos, too valuable to trust to airline luggage, was tucked in my purse where I could touch it for reassurance.

■ ■ ■

I arrived before my flat was ready, so Quinn and Tia brought me to their place in the rural Woolshed Valley, about ten miles outside Beechworth—an appropriately dream-like setting. Apparently inspired by a nautilus shell, Quinn had handcrafted walls of energy-saving mud brick that encircled a kitchen, wound around a wood stove that provided heat, hot water, a stove, and an oven. A small stairway turned up to their sleeping loft. Outside, a subtle network of tubes and gutters saved whatever rain fell on the roofs, separating water for the household from water for the garden, the fruit trees, and grapevines, he explained, knowing I relished every organic detail of his charming, thoughtful creation. A veranda shrouded with grapevines added a touch of tree house to "Thistledew," a name that reflected its whimsical mix of elegant craftsmanship and homestead simplicity.

The grand introductory tour of their property ended at an elegant door crafted of rich red wood. The outhouse was no ordinary hole in the ground but a beautifully enclosed composting toilet, such a startling innovation in the region that the local shire building authorities all came to look it over, Quinn said, his grin revealing how tickled he was by the oddball notoriety of being the first to bring a Clivus composting toilet into rural Victoria.

"Most of the time we don't use the outhouse but simply piddle in the paddock," Tia said.

"The nitrogen is good for the soil," Quinn added, "and the soil here is poor enough that it needs all the help it can get."

After being introduced to their rustic "necessary room," I was eager to share the music I'd brought from America and, unzipping my gigantic teal blue duffel bag, I spilled a rivulet of tapes and CDs across the floor. My little boom box Quinn promptly dubbed R2-D2, as it sang out assurances that it had made the journey safely. But I searched in vain for something else.

"I forgot my underwear," I exclaimed, picturing a small bag I'd left on the bedroom floor half the world away.

"But you brought your music," Quinn chuckled. "I like a woman who has her priorities straight." Our giggles turned into whoops of laughter that continued half the night.

My temporary residence was "LiLi's Flat," the garden guest quarters that often served as a second home for Tia's sister. A constellation of windows, towering ceilings, and a fireplace gave a lavish feel to the quirky mud brick room shaped by Quinn's vision. I slept as if wrapped in a gentle, loving embrace. Awakened by lyrical bird calls, I piddled in the paddock and, wrapped in cool morning mist, watched in disbelief as a mob of kangaroos silently materialized to graze on the hillside.

"You saw the kangaroos!" Tia exclaimed at breakfast. "They're a bit shy and sometimes visitors never do see them."

The kangaroos had welcomed me.

Breakfast—"brekkie"—was a series of astonishing variations on the theme of toast. Crunchy, seed-filled whole wheat bread and thin slices of an ever-so-slightly sweet raisin loaf that exuded a whiff of cinnamon were brought to the lazy Susan at the center of the table to join sweet butter, roasted tahini, honey, and three kinds of jam. Quinn brought out a jar of darkly salty Vegemite, "to show it was a fair dinkum Aussie brekkie," although he confessed he didn't much care for its salty, almost bitter taste. Instead, he demonstrated how to maximize the variations by slicing each piece of toast in quarters, yielding a head-swimming number of possible combinations to be washed down with cups of strong, hot tea.

One morning, Quinn said he'd had a call from his ex. With no fanfare, she decided to send their son, Logan, back to live with his father. Logan, nearly fourteen, was having a turbulent entry into adolescence. "He's always loved living in the Woolshed Valley. He didn't much like living with his mother in Adelaide. After all, he was born right here," Quinn mused. "Maybe reconnecting, walking the hills, and milking the goats will help."

The news rather threw Tia for a loop; she'd raised a daughter, but the mystery of young boys eluded her. "I know it may sound selfish, but I really enjoy life with just the two of us," she confessed. "And while both his kids have stayed with us on school holidays, living together is different."

Only then did I realize my arrival had disrupted their accustomed pattern, too. "Quinn's family has always been more an idea than an everyday reality, while my family has been entwined since the get-go," Tia said. "My sister has lived off and on in the flat out back; my daughter was young when we first got together and lived with us until she got married. His kids have always lived with their mom and just spent a bit of school holidays with us. And until you arrived, I never dreamed I'd have much to do with his American family."

"Funny to be called part of Quinn's American family. To my mind, Quinn and I are both separated from our parents. Him by distance and me by a sort of long-distance estrangement."

"How did that happen? I can't imagine being estranged from my parents," she said. "They're such dears."

"And there's the difference. Mom has a good heart and can

be sweet, but our father? Abrasive and domineering are the words that come to mind," I said.

"Your father's difficult, I'll grant," said Tia. "And one of the nice things about their being in America is, with that distance between us, I don't have to sort out how I feel about any relationship with them," she said with a mischievous giggle. "Is that too awful?"

"Seems just right to me."

Within days, word came that the flat was ready, signaling the end of our getting-to-know-you idyll: Time for Quinn to return to work and for me to begin crafting new living patterns. Quinn dropped me off and drove around back to his workshop; Tia decided to join me for the tour of my new soon-to-be-home, since she hadn't seen the place, either.

Kangaroos stood at attention etched in the glass front doors, offering a metaphoric welcome; I crossed the threshold as if entering a new dream. Half the large, airy entryway was blocked by a curtain of iridescent peacock blue. Pulling it aside, I saw a half-hidden "guest alcove" large enough for a spartan single bed, its head against an archway to nowhere—a blocked-off doorway that bore silent witness to the old house's former glory. Stone walls, freshly painted creamy white, stretched some twelve feet up.

Tia and I opened the bedroom door and burst out laughing at the art deco bed, an island of vintage pink chenille over which dangled an improbably long chain.

"What happens when you yank that?" I asked.

"Maybe this is a special spring-controlled bed that tilts. Pull the chain and you're delivered, feet first, at the foot of the bed, ready to begin your day."

"I thought it might be some special Aussie-designed rip cord. Pull it and you release a hidden mosquito net."

"Maybe it's a way of choosing who you share your bed with."

"Or, perhaps it summons a genie who'll grant you three wishes.

"Or make your dreams come true."

"Only the good ones. Good thing you have the pull chain."

Peering behind the door, we found the far more prosaic answer: The chain turned on a pumpkin-shaped light globe hanging in the corner.

"Now here's a glorious dressing table," Tia said. "As curvy as Jean Harlow—and probably the same vintage. I've never seen one so close to the floor. You have to sit down to see your face in this mirror," she said, playfully demonstrating the proper, lady-like seating to assume the movie magazine gaze into the mirror. "Not to mention, kneeling to open the drawers."

"Handy. Some guy designed this setup."

"Oh, velvet curtains! Just the thing for dust allergies. Do you suppose there's a window behind them?" She tugged aside the weighty tan drapery, revealing a floor-to-ceiling window. "Old wooden blinds, too. Even though it opens onto the veranda. No worry about any stray sunbeam sneaking in," she giggled.

The opposite wall was dominated by an elaborate mantelpiece, its garlands of carved eucalyptus leaves and gum nuts, the remnants of a once-elegant fireplace, now boarded up. We checked to make certain the three wooden wardrobes didn't hold lions or witches. They substituted nicely for closets while barely seeming to fill the cavernous bedroom.

"Maybe this was a dining room, before Rodney carved this old house into apartments," Tia said. "Maybe it matches the lounge room."

"Who's Rodney?" I asked.

"He's your landlord—and Quinn's, too. He's a bit of a miser, likes to scavenge odds and sods.

"Now this shows the Rodney touch," said Tia, stepping

into the living room and surveying its brown plastic chairs and the basic gray Formica and chrome dinette set. The fireplace, which once might have outshone the one in the bedroom, had been transformed into a study in utilitarianism, its frame now ersatz brick, setting off a bulky brown, no-nonsense propane heater.

"Maybe he bought out the remains of an old motel. But he still didn't erase all the charm. That patterned ceiling looks like old pressed tin."

The ceiling rose to a steep peak that held a small, mouth-like vent. "Do the vents stay open all the time?" I asked.

"Lets out the summer heat, though with these thick stone walls, it's hard to imagine this place getting very warm."

"Those moldings looks like carved plaster," I said. "Isn't that almost a lost art here in Australia? I remember stories about a great uncle in Chicago who knew how to do that stuff. He was in demand until he died."

"You have rellies in Chicago?"

"Not any more. Uncle Irving, the master plasterer, has been dead for years. And our grandparents lived in Chicago most of their lives, until Dad insisted they move to Michigan, so he could keep an eye on them."

"Quinn hasn't told me much about that part of family history. I'd love to hear more about them."

"Being the oldest must make me the designated story-keeper and I'll bet I can recall enough to bore your socks off."

"Someday soon let's give that a try," she said, walking through an expansive archway. "This kitchen came from summer camp for elves," she exclaimed, surveying its tiny tin sink and miniature countertop.

"What do elves cook with?" I asked, opening the cabinets

to reveal a neatly stacked set of hopelessly lightweight pans, two cups, four plates, and a few odd utensils.

"A man's eye view of kitchen necessities. But, Di, look at the cook stove."

"Colorado" gleamed across the front in letters of bright chrome.

"It's a message—and Quinn did a lovely job for you. Nice rentals are hard to come by and he's managed to find you a nice, livable spot," she assured me, seeming to intuit how much the flat's cool emptiness made me long for reassurances.

Quinn popped his head in: "No more tourist gawking, we've got to go or we'll be late to rehearsal," he said, looping his arm through Tia's and blowing me a kiss.

I heard their truck crunch away on the gravel. My tears welled up from some deep sadness and the flat echoed with unfinished farewells. If this were a dream, what would it mean? What happens when you live where the living room and the bedrooms are mirror images, separated by an archway opening to a deadend?

As I sat playing with the possibilities of such slightly loony symbolism, suddenly I heard outbursts of compelling, contagious laughter. Kookaburras. Their eerily human hilarity seemed to say, "Lighten up. It's all too funny. Join the party. We're having a bloody marvelous time out here."

Who could resist such an invitation?

Outside I went to stroll around, exploring my newly acquired neighborhood. Down Finch Street, the Beechworth Stagecoach added old mining town color for tourists, and the pair of golden Clydesdales that pulled the crimson carriage added continual plops of steaming manure to keep foot travelers alert.

Beechworth, "The Best Preserved Gold Town in the State of Victoria," according to several plaques on old Victorian stone buildings, was filled with the sort of eclectic gingerbread architecture that would have fit right in to any Rocky Mountain gold mining town—except for the balconies of New Orleans style wrought iron lace. The post office, a small-scale Romanesque fantasy topped with a clock tower, sat in the heart of town, the corner of Ford and Camp Streets, also the stop for the stagecoach, I discovered. I strolled to the Town Hall Gardens, an improbable redwood glade that grew from the vision of an earnest turn-of-the-century botanist who thought Victoria's soft seasons would let exotic trees like California sequoia thrive, another plaque explained. A Victorian gazebo, seemingly snatched from a movie set, served as the bandstand that defined the park center.

Soaring, spiral-branched bunya pines sported metal signs nailed to their trunks to warn the unwary of the danger overhead. Cones the size of pineapples, weighing forty pounds or more, hung ready to clobber any unwary tree jostler.

The indigenous trees are eucalyptus, dozens of varieties, all continually shedding their leaves year-round rather than in a seasonal cycle. I'm entranced to learn that many eucalyptus slough off their bark in fine shreds or two-foot-wide, shield-sized slabs. Trees that shed their skin like snakes speak to me of continual renewal and make visible the subtle link between the underground snake world and the sunlit tree realm above.

Roots cover almost as large an area as the trees above, holding a life force more enduring than the branches. The darkness gives birth to everything striving for sunlight. In touch with root wisdom, a Koori knows just where to reach down and pull out something to eat.

How many times have I, hungry and oblivious, stepped over some underlying nourishment?

Beechworth is a mining town picturesque enough to gladden any film director's heart, with a whiff of the festive and insubstantial about it. I was struck by how much it felt like

Boulder. Walking alongside the icy streams crashing over granite boulders through the center of the town, I slowly realized how Quinn had only partially left Colorado. Squinting at the shapes of the hills around Beechworth, I saw that they could be the Rocky Mountain foothills, although mostly eucalyptus climbed the rocky slopes instead of pines. The way the rocky hills opened to clear, expansive skies, the comforting sense of enduring rocks that encircled and protected, the deliciously crystalline air, all felt utterly familiar.

Quinn had married an Australian girl he'd met in Boulder and, just weeks after their wedding, left for Australia, following the '70s hippie-era dream of living out his Back-to-the-Earth ideals. A young landscaper, in one of life's delicious turnabouts, he was soon working at Canberra's Royal Botanical Gardens, their expert in rare and exotic trees—those being maple, elm, oak, and aspen. But it was in the state of Victoria, so lush that license plates proclaim it "The Garden State," that my brother, the transplanted gardener, had been able to put down his roots.

After journeying halfway around the world, Quinn found a little corner of Australia that most resembled home. The same welcoming spirit whispered to me. I felt a tender thrill pulsing beneath my breastbone, a simple, pagan love that linked me to this kind of countryside as well. As the landscape explained so eloquently, we needed soaring trees, rocky mountains, and clear running streams.

Walking along Beechworth's nearly traffic-less streets, I noticed that most houses have English style names: Lilac Cottage, Kinsroth, Gladstone House. The brass plaque by the door buzzer to my flat says Wimslow.

Wimslow? What does that mean? Have I come on a whim, because I was feeling low? Does it advise slowing my whims?

■ ■ ■

When Joel explained how Koori people know they are children of the earth even before they're born, I felt a humming resonance of recognition. Their web of connections begins when a woman first feels the butterfly flutter of life within her womb: The first quickening is a message from Earth, telling her she's been chosen by the spirit of that place. The subtle internal whisper signals important spiritual tasks. First, she must note exactly where she is in the bush: That spot will always be sacred to the child she carries.

Next, she must locate the nearest sacred site. The bush throbs with sites for women's mysteries and men's rituals, sacred locations that hold different dreamings. If it's sacred to Emu, Black Parrot, or Barramundi, that will be the totem animal of her unborn child. Each Koori comes into the world aware that they have been chosen by their totem animal to guide and share their life journey. As an outsider, I can only marvel at these multi-faceted connections.

Growing up involves ceremonial steps, learning the ways and songs, the laws and the dances of Emu, Parrot, or Kangaroo. The totem animal connection links the realm of the Dreaming and everyday life. Part steward of the land, part game warden, a Koori knows what allows a totem animal to thrive, when it may be endangered, and when it willingly offers itself as food. This teaches a key truth about life in the bush, Joel said: What is sacred to you may be lunch for someone else.

What is often called soul, or life force or spirit, is entwined with one's sacred bit of land in a way that goes deeper than any yearning for home. Often when reaching the end of life, a Koori is brought back to her sacred place and quietly breathes her last with a smile of relaxation and release.

How different my life would be if I'd been told my part in the grand scheme of things was being the guardian of, say, a few acres in the Boulder Valley, if I'd been born knowing I was

Coyote, Prairie Dog, or Trout. Hopelessly romantic, or perhaps filled with holy envy, I yearned for a richer sense of community, one that embraced the welfare of all beings. I could easily look out for the welfare of Coyote if I knew others were equally mindful of Field Mouse and Bobcat, Rattlesnake and Grouse.

Instead, like most modern-day Americans, I'd become nearly immobilized by too much information, overwhelmed by feeling both responsible and powerless.

I had absorbed a tacit assumption of the atmospheric researchers and environmental reporters I worked with—that every problem had a solution, even though each problem extended out in fractal-like expansions when examined closely. Like air pollution, which once seemed the straightforward result of the gunk from cars, trucks, and the stuff burned by power plants. When smokestack filters, catalytic converters, and cleaner-burning fuels cleared the skies, research satellites found that other gases rose up to the stratosphere and ate holes in Earth's invisible ozone umbrella. Pollution's acid fingerprints were found in samples from polar ice caps, cores from the ocean floors, and in clear running Rocky Mountain streams. Large-scale solutions receded into the distance like so many reflections in fun-house mirrors, and I was left composting my garbage and recycling cans, which seemed such a puny response to the thickening pollution along Colorado's Front Range.

Environmental problems grew too large for me to hold in my head. Mining companies planned to excavate along the edge of Yellowstone National Park. Power plants in Utah and New Mexico poisoned creeks along the Continental Divide. Developers poisoned prairie dog colonies to make way for gargantuan houses that gobbled up staggering amounts of wood and metal. Gray whales were dying off Washington's coast while their Mexican nursery lagoons were jeopardized. Snowmobilers chased bison for sport.

Filled with information that spiraled me into an increasingly global despair, I felt powerless to protect the mountains outside my windows. I struggled against feeling immobilized, wrestled with a growing sense of helplessness, while searching for an antidote.

Evenings in the women's circle kept me going, gradually awakening my awareness of Earth as a sacred mystery—a mystery beyond our ability to comprehend. Celebrating the gentle glissade from birth to flowering to death and rebirth filled me with hope. I began rejoicing in the continued promise of each dawn unfolding to mid-day brightness, finding comfort that twilight melted into darkness, which always promised a new day's dawn, sensing a connection with countless people through time who welcomed each day with prayers and blessings. I learned to hear the song echoed in endless variations by trees and birds, people and horses, seals and kelp. I began to feel the energy of Earth as Gaia, a personification of the life force, clad in a swirling blue oceanic dress and gossamer veils of air, jeweled with glaciers, forests, and deserts. I began to see the delicate pavane of clouds, rivers, and lakes as part of a greater cosmic dance.

And I learned to live knowing that if I had spoken about my dreamworld awareness in the lab where I worked, shared my spiritual awakening with colleagues devoted to the rational enterprise of understanding ecosystems, I'd have been dismissed as an utter loon.

■ ■ ■

In Beechworth I faced the mystery of why both Quinn and I had taken root in Fantasy Land "tourist towns"—jumping-off places for vacationers who wanted to escape what's usually called everyday reality—as if living were impossible while surrounded by beauty, as if reality desensitized you to the breathtaking dance of sun and shadows across the landscape, as if the visual feast of mountain streams cascading into canyons were not part of our natural human legacy.

But these "tourist towns" are boundary lands, places with a magical sort of energy that's created where water meets land, where mountains and plains join, where the plants shift and the animals move between one world and another. These may mark the shifts between one climate zone, one ecological niche and its cousin, a place where the soil is dryer, the wind more piercing, but they're also like the "thin places" of Celtic mythology, where only the slightest membrane separates the real world from the magical. This membrane is not only permeable, but it lets the divine mystery glimmer through.

Neither mountains nor flatlands, cities nor wilderness, Beechworth and Boulder may be gateways to other boundaries, places that feel about as close as you can get in Western culture to the land of dreamings. But in truth, this place is Quinn's boundary land, a place where I have no roots.

In Boulder, I kept most of my connections alive with phone calls, but I decided against having a phone at my Finch Street flat out of a simple-minded fear. I was far too accustomed to waiting for it to ring and I didn't want to succumb to my too-familiar pattern of waiting: waiting for the children to fall asleep, waiting for them to understand, waiting for promises to be fulfilled, waiting for things to change, waiting for some invisible, mysterious underground ripening. Wrapped in a peculiar mixture of resignation and helplessness, I smoldered, realizing that somehow, on some level, I had agreed to live life on hold, to wait. Not with excited anticipation nor with a gardener's patience, but with the powerlessness of a prisoner.

Can I learn a new way?

■ ■ ■

On one morning walk, I ventured away from my regular route along the gorge and followed an unexplored bush trail that wound through wattles and eucalyptus to a clearing where I smelled water. I looked around and discovered tiny pools and mossy damp spots filling in pockets on an immense granite rock, which called to me like an ancient grandmother, urging me to come and sit down on a little boulder. Just there, a breathtaking view of a mountain valley opened up. Plants I'd seen nowhere else had taken root in a layer of soil too thin to support any trees. The water tinkled a comfortingly familiar song, wending a trickling path down to the blue-green valley below.

Turning full circle, almost incidentally calling in the powers of the four directions, I saw not a trace of human activity. This little spot of earth had come up to meet me. I felt as if I'd been invited to experience the first day of creation.

"Ingram's Rock" said a little sign by the walking track. Ingram's Rock became the place I could return to for clarity, for solace, for a deeper understanding of my self in this new, upside-down world.

■ ■ ■

Joel explained that when a traveling Koori group arrives at a boundary of another tribe's land where they need permission to cross, they simply sit down and wait. No messages are sent. None are needed. They just wait and an emissary comes.

"How long would somebody be sitting there?" I asked anxiously.

"Not long. Maybe a day," he answered.

I couldn't help wondering if I'd recognize any emissary sent to escort me.

THINGS AND GOODS AND STUFF

Quinn and I shared the same feisty, seventy-some-thing-year-old landlord, Rodney, whose properties include Wimslow and the joinery behind it, a wood-working shop Quinn and his partner share. Stuffed into his tan overalls like an uncooked sausage, Rodney had the bright red complexion that comes to many white Australians who work in the sun. Now a bit of a farmer, he retired from cabinet making by renting the joinery, a corrugated tin structure with the feel of a small barn chockablock with sanders, saws, tools, and cobwebs festooned with sawdust. Adjoining the shop were half a dozen corrugated tin outbuildings. The overflowing sheds, barns, and garages remained Rodney's domain: a platoon of washing machines, assorted barbecues, rusting, unidentifiable fittings. Odd lengths of pipe and scraps of paint-encrusted wood were neatly stacked, sorted by size and mostly under cover. A house-moving trailer and miscellaneous engines kept company with an operational gas pump and the small caravan that served as his second home.

A perpetual garage sale of miscellaneous bits of furniture, glasses, and crockery had a thick layer of dust—to provide inventory control, Quinn said with a grin: Move any object and it leaves a noticeable clear spot. The sheer volume of stuff proclaimed Rodney's dominion over this bit of land.

Storing stuff, not to mention hoarding, is an alien idea to the Koori, as remote as walking on the moon. No family or tribe lingers long in one place because they believe that when people stay in one place, they drain the energy of the earth in that spot. Gathering only what is needed for that day or to be eaten at that moment allows the plants to regenerate so they will be available to feed the people again the next time around.

The junkyard nature of the acre behind my Finch Street flat was mostly concealed; a sign to the Versatile Woodworks gave the only hint that you're in what Quinn calls the heart of Beechworth's industrial district.

A blackboard proclaiming, "No one is at Versatile Woodworks right now, so at the sound of the 'beep' please write your message"—Quinn's response to an increasing dependence on answering machines—hung by the door to the joinery, the largest corrugated tin building around back, where he and his partner, Russ, perform their industrial magic. Their bread-and-butter business comes from building the counters and displays for new stores and shops, although when they restored a Victorian-era grandstand for the National Trust, they also created a community showcase for their restoration skills. But Quinn's true love is crafting custom furniture, like the piano he built for Tia, encasing the workings of an old Steinway in a luscious harmony of woods that asks to be caressed.

Somewhere in the sawdust lurks a glue-spattered phone. When it can be heard over the whine of saws and sanders, it's answered and, if the call is for me, one of the guys comes to fetch me, a system on a par with their chalkboard.

Equally low tech, if not positively retro, was the companionable comfort I got from the radio. The Australian Broadcasting Corp., modeled after England's BBC, unrolled a magic audio carpet, bringing me a full range of music—jazz, classic, world music mixed with new, challenging, hard-toclassify releases. Its news, interviews, and commentaries kept me in touch with the larger world.

A morning program with actors reading parts in a contemporary novel took me back to my childhood, when a pancake-shaped radio under my pillow kept me company as I struggled with asthma and pneumonia. A dime provided phantom radio visitors to entertain me, to connect me with a living, breathing world beyond the crinkling plastic walls of an oxygen tent. Hospitalized for months at a time, I lived through the radio; my life revolved around serials with characters like Ma Perkins and Helen Trent. One show "dared to ask the question, 'Can a girl from the little town of Silver Creek, Colorado, find happiness as the wife of a wealthy and titled Englishman?'" and I dared, too. I explored the Yukon with Sergeant Preston and his dog, King. Programmed to smell the ocean and feel salt spray by the creak of a sailboat's rigging or the flap of a canvas sail, I easily ventured into vivid imaginal worlds.

Whether it was Robert Bly in person, strumming his balalaika and crooning, "We're leaving this time now," or the ABC theme music announcing the serial reading of *Crossing to Safety,* some part of me still fills with anticipation at any invitation to storytelling time.

■ ■ ■

More than a week into my stay, I'm stumped. Can't figure out what I really need and what I simply miss. Scant, unfamiliar items in Beechworth's grocery and the tiny mercantile store contrast sharply with memories of the over-abundance of goods at home.

Goods: What an intriguing meaning. Things make life good. Living with fewer goods is an un-good (if not downright bad) existence. Deprivation equals depravity, or something like that. With less stuff, less stuffing, one feels empty.

Stumbling over ways that language shapes my unconscious assumptions, directing my thinking just below the awareness radar, I realize this echoes observations Thoreau made more than a century ago.

Getting by with few material possessions is one way to cleanse, un-stuff, and leave behind the sensory overload of life in Boulder, I told myself. But noble sentiments aside, cooking, eating, and minimal housekeeping required more than I could cram into my two allotted suitcases. Tia provided pot holders, towels, and a set of sheets. Quinn's scavenging turned up a Formica kitchen table for writing, a dish drainer only slightly the worse for wear, and a discarded table top transformed into a makeshift lounge room coffee table. Finding a bedside reading light in a secondhand shop salved my anti-consumer conscience. But what's a kitchen without a frying pan, a salad bowl, or a single empty jar?

Camping out, mid-way between transient and settled, I recognized the reflex to reconstruct what I left behind and decided to try to sidestep making a one-for-one replacement of every aspect of my life. Much beyond that, I was lost.

Gardens offer a tangible metaphor for absorbing this new place. A happy collision of British culture and down-under exotica creates riotous gardens: palm trees next to roses, wisteria and wild hops vines entwining eucalyptus. The elaborate songs of unknown birds underscore the waves of strangeness as I walk Beechworth's quiet streets.

On the heels of each observation comes the realization that what's new to me is utterly unremarkable to everyone else. With no one to share my delight in discovering the obvious, all my ideas and observations, mullings, and musings bubbled away inside.

Time to begin writing. Not in journalist mode, nor as the science writer, but more as an explorer, following emotional roots, learning to trace their invisible energy patterns. Tracking these emerging song lines, sharing the search, would keep me connected with the women's circle, I thought. Trying to find a computer prompted another new adventure.

Innately suspicious of electronic gadgets, Quinn asked, "Why do you need a computer? You're a writer. All you need is a paper and pencil."

"You're a carpenter. All you need is a hammer, a saw, and a chisel. Why do you need all those fancy tools you have back in your workshop?"

No further quibbles. He obligingly scouted up a bloke preparing to open a Macintosh store in Albury, less than an hour's drive away.

Intrigued by a call from a displaced Yankee in the Victoria hills, Andy, the soon-to-be manager, listened sympathetically as I explained that I'd not brought along my computer because of the differences between American and Australian electrical current, then offered to deliver a secondhand Mac with a jaunty, "No worries, mate." His store was not yet ready to open, his family had just moved up from Melbourne, and he'd heard Beechworth was a charming place for an outing.

We set a time on Saturday morning. The appointed hour went by and then another. Just as I was getting worried, a car pulled onto the footpath and Andy emerged smiling and apologetic. With my accent, he thought I had said "seventeen" Finch Street and when the people at 17 Finch Street didn't know me, at 71 Finch Street, he was stymied.

But Saturday is market day in every rural town, his wife remembered, so off they went to the grocery store. Sure enough, the second person they asked said, "Oh, Quinn's sister!" and gave them directions to the flat by the "Versatile Woodworks" sign.

One fact of small-town life—a resident of less than a week, I'm already known.

■ ■ ■

The town may know me, but can I reciprocate? The Australia Day ceremony in the Town Hall Gardens would provide a brilliant introduction to life in Beechworth, said Logan, his fourteen-year-old enthusiasm ignited because he and two Boy Scout mates were in charge of lowering the flag to mark the end of the event. Australia Day is a celebration of statehood, sort of a combination of the Fourth of July and Columbus Day, Quinn explained, helping to bridge the cultural gap. Only later did I discover that the grim implications of Australia Day for the Koori people mirrored what Columbus Day now means for Native Americans.

Nearly a hundred people gathered for the ritual. A beaming redheaded young matron, standing proud in a tightly fitting scout uniform, was proclaimed "Beechworth Citizen of the Year." Others who had earlier been given medals from the state of Victoria were honored, including a well-known writer and a musician, both friends of Quinn and Tia. Oddly touching to recognize people for simply being good at what they do or who they are, for contributing to the community by being themselves. The opportunities for positive recognition are much harder to come by in the U.S. Even the opportunity to try your hand at something new—without gathering credentials, qualifications, or experience—is more scarce—one of the reasons Quinn opted for Australia.

As the flag was lowered, it snagged momentarily on the stone park gateway. Catching the flag without letting it touch the ground for even a moment, then folding it perfectly, the boys did their bit to end the solemn ceremony. Afterward,

Logan beamed with a mixture of relief and pride and, waving me toward the picnic tables, dashed off with his mates.

Plates of "nibbles"—cold cuts, salads, sliced pickled beets, watermelon, and other picnic fare—appeared out of baskets and portable coolers as I, the obvious stranger, elicited inquisitive looks. Introducing myself as Quinn's sister gave me admittance, established a link, so I'm not simply a nosy-beak stranger who happened into the park in time to help herself to the goodies. A group called the Homemakers organized the food ritual, said one of the women guarding a picnic table. Other aged Homemakers chimed in, describing the pickled beet root salad, an especially tangy cheese, and the homemade mustard. With the enthusiasm shared by cooks everywhere, they introduced me to an unfamiliar dessert called damper: plain soda bread topped with butter and lightly flavored Golden Syrup. Usually cooked over a camp stove, damper is a portable, homey treat, they explained. Sorry, the Golden Syrup was already gone.

A large black dog stealing a bone from an ancient fox terrier provided the only ruffle on the calm surface of the afternoon as sweet and golden as the tinned syrup. Children snatched the last few bites of fruit salad, the women dusted grass and crumbs from their house dresses and packed up the last picnic basket.

■ ■ ■

Quinn, as fond of good food as I am, had spent years searching out the tasty bits among all the local shops and restaurants that seemed mostly to specialize in colonial variations on English pub food. The British approach to food, dubious at best, generally hasn't been improved upon hereabouts, he observed, warning me away from the tasteless "poyes" and "dim sims" from the local milk bar. Some of the food can be so appalling that he will take a detour if the one acceptable place is closed; some small rural towns he avoids altogether.

Though he's scoped out the culinary landscape, some treats he still missed—like chocolate brownies. Befriending the local baker, Quinn described the taste, texture, and consistency of the brownies he remembered from home, resulting in pan after experimental pan yielding variations on a chocolate cake theme. One has since become a big seller for the Beechworth Bakery, and Quinn has learned, out of longing and gastronomic desperation, to devise a reasonable approximation of brownies in the circular kitchen of Thistledew, where he does most of the cooking.

I'd forgotten the easy way Quinn and I pottered around in the kitchen when we lived together after my divorce, sharing the small daily tasks of food making until one day, with obvious excitement, Tia and Logan announced that Quinn was going to make his special split pea soup.

"What's so special about this pea soup?" I asked, joining Quinn in chopping onions and carrots.

"It's the recipe you taught me years ago. You told me that, since I'd decided to be a vegetarian and, given my interests, was probably not going to make a lot of money, I'd jolly well better learn how to make pea soup," he recalled, describing the kitchen and even remembering who shared that meal.

Until then, I hadn't realized the strength of the ties Quinn and I had forged over the cutting board, the sink, and the stove. We share a deep response to the meditative quality of chopping and the sensuous thrill of crushing fresh dill or garlic. The simple gratitude that wells up feeling the skin of an eggplant or the gentle firmness of a tomato is a shared satisfaction that time and distance had thickened like a slowly simmering sauce.

Food was woven into the daily patterns of the Koori people, too, enriching their ties with each other in ways I can only guess. Strolling across the landscape, a band of Koori would have moved slowly, chatting or singing, keeping a comfortable pace for the small children, each woman's hip holding a coolamon, a wooden gathering bowl, in her hand a digging stick. Casually focusing on the surrounding bush, attuned to what may offer itself as food, they collected most of the tribe's food with less than three hours of gathering a day. Babies were carried until they could walk, cradled in coolamons that have been softened with leaves or moss that served as organic disposable diapers.

By the time they become toddlers, Koori children, accustomed to the daily patterns of gathering, feed themselves with the complete ease of independence. They effortlessly learned about finding and caring for food; gathering tasty bush morsels, while always leaving enough for the next season, is second nature.

"Put a white man down in the desert and he'll starve to death," says Joel. "For us, it's like being dropped off at the supermarket.

"We often say that one of the reasons white men are so mean is because they don't know how to feed themselves."

■ ■ ■

I was surprised to discover that I'd unwittingly enrolled in a life-movement laboratory. Even the smallest muscles and neurons had to relearn an unexpected array of embedded patterns. Accustomed to flipping on the light when I entered a room, instead I had to pat down half the wall fumbling for a maddeningly tiny switch, smaller than a pencil eraser, mounted near eye level; once it was located, the next challenge became deciding what to do when "off" is up and down is "on." Doorknobs and latches located either knee-high or level with my nose forced me to lurch into the store and stumble into the bank. I groped like a blind woman at the lock on the door of my Finch Street flat.

Kitchen cupboards and counters, even the cups and spoons, seemed sized for a playhouse, rendering me the giant Alice after eating the mushroom. Burners on the propane stove had to be lit from a particular angle and electric outlets came with individual switches, so I constantly found myself thinking I'd started heating water in the jug only to realize I'd turned on the toaster—which needed close watching or it became an incinerator. Giant, absent-minded Alice, amazed at the simple, second-nature movements that no longer worked.

British-style driving induced a distressing dyslexia. Walking to an intersection, I didn't know which way to look or how to anticipate the direction a turning car would take. A stumble-bum even as a passenger, I inevitably went to the wrong side of a car and then managed to stand in the wrong place for the door to open.

Beechworth's wide streets had so little traffic that one morning Quinn gave me the keys to drive his truck downtown, with Logan beside me as guide and driving coach. Shifting gears with my left hand and relegating my right to tripping the turn signals offered another set of challenges.

"Turn left," Logan said as we reached the intersection.

Brain and body froze simultaneously.

"Please, just point," I muttered, panicked by my apparent dyslexia. He obliged, and I swung left, guiding the balky truck to the right—and completely incorrect—side of the road.

"Wrong side!" he yelled, laughing at my awkwardly exe-cuted mid-block correction. With more giggling prompts, we made it to the store and back without mishap. "That was as good as a carnival ride," he exclaimed, clearly relishing my four-wheeled befuddlement.

I said a quick prayer of thanks for whatever wisdom guided me to accept the limits of living without a car in the land of looking-glass driving.

And another prayer to hurry along some new right-left neural connections, so my brain could cope with crossing the streets without panic.

GREENING

"Interested in a little day trip?" Tia asked as the January weather turned from spring-like to balmy. Robin, one of her private music students, had proposed we join her in a quest: finding Green Pharm, a place she'd only heard about. Meeting Robin, a sixty-ish woman who'd been widowed for about a year, would be a treat in itself, Tia confided, even though no one knew much about Green Pharm. We planned to gather at my flat early the next day.

The doorbell squawked, announcing an elfin woman with mischief dancing in her bright brown eyes and a face shaped by mirth and good humor. Petite and appropriately bird-like, Robin introduced herself and then led me outside for introductions to Roma, her tiny white car.

"No need to fuss about food; I've got a picnic lunch tucked in the boot," she said, flashing a smile that revealed a gypsy-like glimmer of gold. The rich, plummy tones of her proper English schooling signaled me to observe the conventional rules of decorum and restraint, even though I really wanted to throw my arms around her and exclaim, "Oh, Hooray! Hooray! Here you are at last!" I was surprised by the companionable connection I felt the instant her brown eyes joined her smile.

Quinn and Tia arrived, filling Roma to capacity, and we headed into the bush as Robin detailed the adventure du jour —sussing out Green Pharm.

"Sulfur-crested cockies," said Robin as I gaped in amazement when a white cloud of golden-crested cockatoos burst open, wheeling and squawking. Coalescing into an animated fringe topping every branch of a towering white bark gum tree, these dazzling birds I'd seen only in zoos took a brief pause in their aerial acrobatic routine.

Robin spun a sparkling narrative as we bumped along the remote, dusty track, spangled by the sunburst joy of following her own idiosyncratic bliss at last. "They're clever larrikins who consider agriculture one of the greatest jokes," she said with an appreciative chuckle. "Agriculture is an uncomfortable fit for much of this landscape and the cockatoos have devised special tricks to infuriate farmers—like following behind them as they're sowing, feasting on the seed as fast as they lay it down, laughing and carrying on as they enjoy the treats fortune provides."

Accustomed to a universe that freely provided food, Koori people, too, had similar difficulties in distinguishing between providence and the alien ideas of agriculture and private property; when lucking upon a stray sheep wandering in the bush, it seemed no different than finding a kangaroo, and in earlier times, farmers greeted Koori and cockatoo with rounds of buckshot.

The cockatoo cloud swirled again as they chased each other, the shadows of cloud scudding across the rolling hills and, with a final comic flourish, the cockies dived after the car's rooster tail of dust. I was still laughing at their playful antics when we arrived at the cool glen that held Green Pharm.

"Cockatoos are the buffoons, the rowdies of the bird world," said Tom, head honcho, chief gardener, and resident herbalist, less than impressed with the cockatoo acrobatic display. "If they were human, they'd be speeding around in loud cars, swilling beer, tossing cans out the window, swearing and ogling passing girls.

"None of the Australian birds migrate; they simply go where there's good tucker," he added, reflexively grumpy at the cockies' raucous squawking, although clearly his thriving herb acreage had suffered no harm.

Leading an impromptu tour, Tom strode between plots of herbs at a remarkable clip, explaining the conditions of soil and light each needed to thrive. "Dandelions?" I exclaimed, startled by one carefully tended patch. "You cultivate dandelions? Don't they grow everywhere?"

"Both their leaves and roots are useful for immune and nervous system disorders as well as for regulating the body's blood and digestion," Tom said, eyeing his Yankee visitor for the unobservant dunce she'd revealed herself to be, "and they don't grow here all by themselves," nodding toward the edge of his vibrant oasis. Miles of scrub and dusty eucalyptus stretched to the horizon, their hard-edged leaves gently clattering with a hint of a breeze.

Were healing and medicinal plants appropriate agriculture for the Australian bush? What scale of chemistry was needed to transform flowers to pharmaceuticals? As Tom toured us through the small, sparkling laboratory and the computer his little enterprise used to reach a national market, Robin peppered him with questions.

Sharing a picnic lunch and a bit of our personal stories, Robin and I both reveled in the delicious paradox of finding a new acquaintance who, as if by magic, came with a built-in sense of comfort. We webbed together a sparkling new companionship, comparing notes about healing plants interspersed with snippets of our lives, and she told me a bit about living in rural Denmark and then in a small town in the Andes. Once she, her husband, and sons arrived in Australia, she quickly found work with a center settling new immigrants and, while her sons were young, she'd funneled her fact-gathering energies into writing and producing a series of radio programs. For Robin, widowhood had released her from half a lifetime of suppressed vitality. With the bright-eyed wonder of the independent scholar soaring beyond classroom constraints, Robin couldn't hide her quirky, contagious curiosity even if she'd wanted to—and I was grateful that she didn't. After drinking in a newfound connection, the healing gardens, the sun-spangled day, I was returned to my doorstep with a satisfied fullness—and the realization that I hadn't acknowledged that I was lonely.

"Drop by my house some day soon," she said, giving me directions to her A-frame overlooking Lake Sambell. Not sure what would appear too eager, I waited a couple of days before walking over.

Robin's cozy lair overlooked Lake Sambell and Temple Street, and both preserved bits of Beechworth's legacy, she explained as she toured me through her little domain. "A hundred years ago, perhaps half the souls in Beechworth were Chinese—miners, cooks, and laborers," she said. "This hill had been the site of their temple—but with the mines and no lake, it didn't look like much then. Lots of Chinese fortune seekers flocked to Victoria, drawn by dreams of riches. Everyone hoped to find an easy way to the gold and silver locked in the local granite."

The Chinese, skilled in carving sluices and watercourses from bedrock, were welcomed mostly as laborers, not partners in the rough-and-tumble frontier ventures. For example, the small stone building called the Powder Magazine, a local landmark, was built to keep the Chinese from taking the gunpowder to make firecrackers, Robin explained.

Mining-era relics mark many of Beechworth's undulating hills. Sluices carved into the gray, tan, and pink boulders sped the water by straightening out its serpentine meanders, transforming the watercourses into mining tools. The altered stream spills into a gorge too steep to be tamed. The gorge is now a nature sanctuary crisscrossed with walking trails. A "gorge view" offers a prized taste of pristine bush, enhancing the value of a cottage or a bed-and-breakfast. A two-minute walk took me from my flat to the wallaby-tested trails that fringe the gorge.

■ ■ ■

One evening after supper, Quinn, Tia, and I stepped from the Hibernian Pub into the apricot light of a dazzling, splashy-orange sunset. "Hop into the truck and we'll get a better view," he said, heading for the drive that skims down into the gorge. By the time we reached a scenic overlook, Quinn was disappointed that the sunset colors were fading and I was giggling.

"Why are you laughing?" he grumbled.

"Back in Boulder, when we want to see a sunset, we head for a higher place, not a lower one," I laughed, unaware that Quinn's perspective had shifted; his focus was down and inward; my perspective was still up and out. I'd not yet learned to listen to the landscape. But I kept exploring, walking, and learning to listen.

■ ■ ■

It seemed like each new landscape brought a new lesson. A short walk from my flat, across from the gorge, twin stone towers, roofed in gleaming Chinese red, loomed more than ten feet above the gateway to Beechworth's cemetery, guarding the cemetery's flank from motorists on the road to Yackandandah. Charred niches still bore open-mouthed witness to those who burned money and prayers so that the smoke would carry good fortune and fond wishes to accompany the dead on their final journey. The orderly white headstones, calligraphy nearly obscured by time, witness the phantom presence of more than three thousand Chinese people who had to be laid to rest so far from their homes. Neatly divided into sections, the rest of the Beechworth cemetery is designated "Church of England," "Presbyterian," "Roman Catholic," and, my favorite, "Strangers." There, the old grave markers revealed a Sikh, an Afghani, and an Indian from Madras among the departed newcomers, but the cold stone markers gave no clues about the dreams that entwined with their fates.

The very idea of a cemetery is alien to the Koori, Joel explained. Occasionally, they buried their dead, but they might be set afloat in a dugout canoe or wrapped in a fetal position and nestled inside a hollow tree. "'Inconsistent funeral practices' provided further evidence of the 'primitiveness' of the Koori people, as far as European anthropologists were concerned," he said, not bothering to strip the sarcasm from his voice.

As death approached, tribal elders chose special people from one's totem clan to serve as guardians or guides and help with the final steps of one's journey. Often simply returning to the spot of the earth that had given them life created a spiritual homecoming; coming full circle insured a peaceful release. Relaxing into a gentle letting go, one's soul returned to the Dreaming. The guardians decided what sort of burial would help complete that person's soul work: Being cast adrift, laid to rest inside a tree, or placed by a special rock, each helped shape the soul's journey in a different way. To the Koori, the white man's "one size fits all" burials seemed shockingly bar-

baric—a soul-less disregard for each individual's uniqueness. I was struck by the irony of the dominant culture, so proud of valuing individuality, while contenting itself with such bland, homogenized rituals to mark one of life's great mysteries.

I recalled Ysaye Barnwell's explaining that some spirituals, like "Swing Low, Sweet Chariot," provided the rhythm to ease a person's dying with a pace that calmed labored breathing and eased a weary soul's release. And the idea of having loving companions beside you when facing the mystery of death felt comforting and appropriate. I remembered that Helen, the crone of our circle, prepared for her death when she reached eighty-four, visiting every person she had ever had difficulties with. None of us knew that was her plan. Maybe she wasn't conscious of it, either. "But when she insisted on visiting her sister-in-law, out of state, I knew something was up," her daughter said. Helen returned from that trip on a Friday, entered the hospital on Saturday, and died on Sunday, her life completed. I like to believe I would trust my circle of women friends to decide what's best for my soul. Expanding our connections to face the last, great mystery seems such a natural extension of the ways I treasured their caring, trusted their advice, and valued their collective wisdom.

Walking among the graves of strangers, I longed to talk about this final mystery in the circle with my soul sisters— but they were halfway around the world. Instead, I argued with one ever-so-familiar voice inside my head, the one that continually argues for wariness when faced with the unknown. Letting yourself get comfortable is an invitation to disaster, it cautions; it's not safe to let your guard down, to yield to believing, to trust wordless feelings, to forget the possibility of danger or betrayal. Remember Inana's journey down under, it murmured; don't forget that innocent trust begins the oldest story in the world.

But what if it's my own mistrustful vigilance, the ambiguous wariness that keeps me looking over my shoulder, that actually invites calamity?

Breathe deeply, stay calm, and look inside, I told myself as I headed back from the cemetery. A sudden wind gusted up with scents of eucalyptus, pine, horses, petrol, the ripe, dusty aroma of the bush—almost perfume, not quite. Low clouds encircled the horizon, dissolving the sun in foggy hills of gray as the restless night descended. The wind howled and moaned, then drum-drum-drummed the blinds against Wimslow's stone walls. The shutters added a tinny tink-tink—almost music, not quite. Then overhead, the center of the sky slowly cleared; the stars emerged one by one, humming chords I strained to hear.

As stars filled the sky with constellations I'd never seen before, I gradually let their light reconnect me with the larger mystery, reminding me that this life was a gift to be savored—joys, goose bumps, and all.

MAGPIES AND MAGIC

My body tingled and my imagination soared the first time I heard the unworldly sounds of Australian magpies. Their warbling acrobatics, like pan pipes played under water, or perhaps a chorus of aeolian harps made liquid, were so astonishing that I had to look two, three, then four times to believe the extravagant arias I was hearing emerged from ordinary-looking black and white birds. I couldn't help smiling at the joyful incongruity of these generically colored critters weaving sun, clouds, and sky into breathtaking sound; remembering the decidedly unglamorous squawks of parrots and the peacock's unnerving cries reminded me that there's little relationship between a bird's appearance and the glory of its song. But I needed to know more about these magpies that differed so from their namesakes in Colorado. All the magpies I had known were long-tailed scavengers who reluctantly flew away from road kill, cursing any oncoming vehicle with crow-like caws.

Native legends say that Magpie created the dawn, so today's magpies still celebrate that feat by renewing their claim to ownership, greeting each Australian dawn with extravagant exuberance. Magpie concerts call me to mindfulness mixed with joy, a reminder to open my arms to each new dawn, to be grateful for the renewal each day brings and treasure its power to surprise. In some mysterious way, magpie songs gave me a vivid taste of the Koori's love of the earth, their yearning to see it as it was at the Dawn of Creation; somehow the cells of my body knew the reason for ending a tribal ritual by backing away from a sacred site, erasing their traces, sweeping away their footprints with emu feathers.

The spell of Australian bird songs seems to be permanent. I now listen to them on a treasured tape and sometimes find myself renting Aussie movies just to hear the maggies sing in the background; their chorus renews my excitement for the daily promise of creation. They inspire an ardor that shows up in the oddest ways, but one shared by the women in the circle. One evening in the circle when Nancy exclaimed, "The whole world would be better off if men simply learned to clean up their own messes." A research scientist, she knew firsthand of the legacy of those unattended messes on a global scale: grotesquely mis-shapen fish, dead lakes, tainted air, and toxic streams.

Nancy's clarity emboldened me to bring this simple idea outside the circle and challenge a scientist reviewing my draft of a news story. "You say 'man-made pollution,' when, as a feminist, you should say 'caused by human activities.' You wouldn't want to exclude women, would you?" he demanded, half teasing, half confronting.

"In truth, I want to exclude women, in this instance. We'll include women when the steel mills and manufacturing com-panies are mostly controlled by women, when trucks and cars are made by women-owned businesses, and when women run the mines and tunnel through the mountains. But right now, men's activities are responsible for the lion's share of the mess."

He shrugged and left with no reply.

■ ■ ■

A rain shower flushed clouds of bugs from my Finch Street yard, and finches, robins, wrens, and miniature willy wagtails swooped down to a bounteous lunch—and I wondered about their taking in a dose of toxins with it. "Are there chemicals in the gardens?" I asked Quinn. "Not enough to worry about," he said. "But it's not out of any heightened environmental awareness. Australians just aren't as house proud as Americans, so even in the cities they don't heap tons of chemicals on their lawns." And, he added with a grin of complicity, "out here in the countryside, house standards are even more lax." The changing bouquet of birds rejoiced, and I relinquished my weed-killer worries.

■ ■ ■

No cause for worry. As the chorus of birds warbled and the sun climbed the sky beyond my veranda, Beechworth hummed in the calm embrace of everyday living, gently paced. Even the ambulances next door glided quietly on their missions. No wailing sirens.

No cause for worry about the yappy dogs I encountered along the footpaths. "They're just extended doorbells," said an old man as we met along a gorge track. "The dogs bark to announce that someone's on the road. You just acknowledge they've done their job and tell them to stop the racket and hush up, just like every other person in their lives does. Then they accept you and let you pass in peace."

I began exploring more beyond the town's boundaries. Walking toward Red Hill along one dusty gravel track, I turned at a sign announcing a nature preserve. The familiar mountain surf murmur of wind in the pines, the crunch of gravel under my feet, the whoosh of birds all lulled me. At least an hour had passed with no sign of another soul, not even the distant rumble of a car bouncing along the rock-strewn road. As the day grew warmer and the sun climbed higher, feeling both comfortable and bold, I took my shirt off. The sun, the tang of pine caressed my shoulders and breasts as I savored the forbidden sweetness of uncovering, giving myself over to daydreams.

In our dreams, rocks can vibrate with emotional numinousness and still retain their solid rockness. A waterfall may sing of creative outpourings, reveal that something hidden is bursting to the surface, while still holding water's primal promise to cleanse and refresh. Shifting meanings, glissading from one level to another, are part of living in dreamtime, I realized. The Dreaming is a metaphor to evoke what happens when you see with your inner eyes and listen with mind and heart open.

I began daydreaming, wondering if the Koori people once walked this hill with only sunlight cloaking their experienced skin. Did the knowing breeze riffle each hair with the taste of distant water, the dusty kiss of pine pollen?

Pine pollen? Listening to what my body had observed yanked me abruptly from my reverie. Pine trees are not native to Australia, I remembered. So why were there only pine trees hereabouts? Focusing on the oddity, I stepped off the track and suddenly saw what the lush underbrush had camouflaged— the interloping conifers had been planted in regimented rows. My dreamy connections with those who once walked the landscape sprang up in the artificial environment of a pine plantation just about ready for harvesting.

I had to laugh. So much for my being in touch with the subtle rhythms of the earth.

CIRCLE UP

Moslems say that the human soul can only travel as fast as a galloping camel—which is my favorite explanation for jet lag. It was winter when I left Boulder, flew for more than twenty-four hours, and arrived in Australia's summer—on the same day I'd left. Recovering from the time-travel required waiting for my soul in more ways than I could have imagined, however. After nearly twenty years of weekly meetings with my women's circle, I had been subtly altered by staying in touch with the Solstices and Equinoxes and the cross-quarter days in between. Ripped away from the rhythm of night and day and thrust from winter's cool contemplation into the expansive energy of Australian spring, I was also dislocated in Earth's seasonal cycles.

I'd been dropped like a stitch in the net of time.

When I was a child, time seemed linear—a flimsy, translucent thread extending into infinity, anchored to nothing. The women's circle had transformed my sense of time from an unspooling thread to a web of connections. Knowing our own life cycles mirrored Earth's continuously repeating cycles, from spring to summer to winter, from beginning to middle to end, gave me a deep, rich comfort. Watching, feeling, sensing how much of our own lives echoed the shift from maiden to mother to crone provided a reassuring pattern beyond the day-to-day chaos. The year was a circle, I realized, a wheel that slowly turned from the Winter Solstice to Spring

Equinox, from Summer Solstice to the Autumnal Equinox. As I began relaxing into my own small place in the grand scheme of things, I gradually moved into a partnership with time.

■ ■ ■

Now it's embarrassing to recall how long it took me to recognize the power of the circle—something indigenous people have known since the beginning of time. The Lakota say that the power of the world lives in circles, all things becoming round. It's only when we sit in circles that we can all speak with each other from our hearts. In the Native American tradition, in circles, we're all equal; in circles, we can all face each other—and ourselves.

In the Koori women's humming dot paintings, circles mark the waterholes, campsites, and gathering places. Circles show the sacred spots where the spirit of each place emerges. Plains Indians made round tepees, so their homes were like the nests of their brothers and sisters, the birds. Navajo prefer their round hogans because rectangular dwellings have corners where evil spirits can congregate. People around a campfire, or a group of women encircling candles, are tapping into the primal power of circles.

I grew up with a language that says you go around in circles when you're lost or crazy, frightened or confused. But for me, it was just the opposite—it was in circles that I found myself.

Earth revolving on its axis slowly encircling the sun traces the large, enduring circles that silently support our own day-to-day confusion. Each day reminds us of a circle, with its regular progression from dawn to noon to twilight then darkness that gives way to a new dawn. The days lengthen and shorten in reassuring repetition as all of Mother Earth's creatures—the peripatetic people as well as the plants and the trees—trace their own cycles, from emergence to bloom, from autumn harvest to winter sleep. While transient typhoons may roar across the seas and earthquakes make the continents tremble, Earth's gentle cycles continue. Even the whales and fish, the algae and plankton, the ocean tides and deep upwellings undulate in cyclical rhythm. Each atom's particles orbit in primal circles, tiny echoes of the sun, the earth, the planets and stars.

First there were the talking circles that in the early '70s we called consciousness raising or CR groups—regular gatherings of women committed to exploring our role in society, our relationships with men, with other women, with our deeper selves, raising our conscious awareness of many of our culture's unexamined ideas and behavior patterns. Then came ritual circles of men and women and teaching circles, all spiraling toward our women's circles, each preserving the primal pattern as old as time. Within the circle, I felt the stately rhythms of the shifting seasons, filling my life with a new richness. My gratitude expanded gently outward like ripples across a pond. In the women's circle, the shift of the seasons and movement of the wheel of the year gave us ways to connect with the rhythms our bodies already knew, the shape our lives silently followed beneath conscious knowing. The continuous circle showed us the larger undulations of our lives.

With hindsight, it seems no coincidence whatsoever that Les, my only Native American lover, was the one who first gave me a wheel of the year, drawn with mathematical precision and divided into fifty-two weeks. Marked with the Equinoxes and Solstices, as well as the mid-points between them, the cross-quarter days, his extraordinary gift helped me, quite literally, to see time through far more ancient eyes.

And then I forgot what I knew. Caught up in the mundane details of preparing to leave Boulder, I'd overlooked how traveling to the antipode would upend my connection with

Earth, assuming that part of my life would simply take care of itself. Paying attention to the urgent while overlooking the important—how many times must I circle around and encounter that particular lesson in order to learn it?

Time traveler with no map or compass, I suddenly realized that I—the one who'd yet to master the time shifts between Boulder and Beechworth in order to call Quinn at a decent hour—now had to puzzle out my place in the seasons on the other side of the world.

Quinn and I had watched Tia struggle to understand our explanation of seasonal cycles of vegetation in the northern hemisphere. "Oh!" she exclaimed as the penny dropped, "That's why you call it 'fall!' All the leaves—they fall down." We couldn't help laughing at our own obtuseness. We'd never stopped to think that a winter landscape of naked trees was an alien experience. A native Australian, Tia grew up surrounded by eucalyptus, trees that grow and shed their leaves continually.

Nearly February. That meant the northern hemisphere days were growing longer after Winter Solstice. By the first of February we can begin to notice that the sun lingers a bit before going below the horizon. Old Celtic calendars call this cross-quarter day Candlemass, Imbolc, and Brigit's Day. In America, it's called Groundhog Day.

Australia had passed the Summer Solstice. My mind balked at the twistings and turnings, so I grabbed a pencil and paper to sketch out the wheel of the year. Autumnal Equinox was approaching but first came the cross-quarter day of Lammas, or Lugnasad, the time when the sun's power, in full summer glory, begins to fade. I'd come into the dying part of the year.

■ ■ ■

For most of my adult life, the calming strength of the women's circle had brought me back to emotional center.

Knowing that one evening a week I'd be with my skin sisters kept me going the other days. Our handcrafted rituals restored my connection with Earth's seasonal changes, recalling—sometimes with awe, sometimes with sadness, often with hilarious, whooping joy—the steady natural rhythm of our lives. After weeks down under, I finally recalled how often my feeling empty or afraid melted away in the circle's familiar calmness.

So out of touch with myself that I couldn't decide which hemisphere's seasons could be my guide, I felt a bit naked, powerless, and uncertain with no other women to help create a circle. But on the wall of my flat I spied the lovely moon-phase calendar Yvonne had given me at Solstice. I sighed with relief; at least the moon was the same. The calendar revealed it was the dark of the moon, the time for planting deep and sewing seeds; I remembered how to reconnect with the dark mother moon.

There was nothing to do but begin. That usually meant lighting a candle in the center of the circle, rekindling the primal, everyday magic, becoming equal parts of the whole circle. The center candle, the mother candle, illuminated a place where we could shed the day-to-day frazzles and recall our connections with each other and, often, our higher, brighter, more loving selves.

Alone, I lit a candle in the center of my lounge room, marveling at how it created a welcoming circle of dancing light. Lighting candles in the four directions, invoking the elements of earth, air, fire, and water, we called on the elemental powers to create a safe space for us to share and explore, learn and grieve, laugh and grow.

Starting in the East, the direction of dawn and new beginnings, I lit the candles, marveling at how different it felt to have the South be the source of storms and severe weather; the

North the direction of the warming, benevolent sun; grateful that the West remained the place of closure, of sunsets, the gateway to the dreaming dark.

The simple ritual of lighting a circle of candles opened me to my tears and began transforming the empty place inside me into a more sacred space, a waiting womb rather than an echoing hollow. Recalling the universal way that trees connect the upper and lower worlds, transforming air, sun, and water to wood and root, leaf and branch, prompted me to begin the tree meditation. I began feeling my feet as roots that dug deeper, down through the living rock to the liquid fire at the center of the earth. My roots drew up the fiery power of Earth, and I felt it rise up through my feet and legs, my body, my trunk; I felt the strength of the molten rock move up, through my body and out the top of my head. The crown of my head grew branches and became the crown of a tree, with limbs reaching up, sensing every breeze, stretching toward the sun. Soaking in the sun's energy, the source of all life, my branches reached way up and stretched far out, then swept down, touching the earth, making a circuit, completing the circle. Once I could feel the energy flowing through me, the sun's warmth gently pouring over me, I could begin reclaiming my place on earth.

Self-consciously at first, I began one of our comforting chants:

> Ancient Mother, I hear you calling
> Ancient Mother, I see your smile
> Ancient Mother, I hear your laughter
> Ancient Mother, I taste your tears.

As I began to feel and hear each word, each sound rang with the recollection of the familiar voices, as I felt the loving embrace of the women of the circle. Each note vibrating through my bones and sinews seemed to slow the flow of blood through my body, altering my pulse to the chant's contemplative pace.

I remembered learning this from the wise woman Starhawk—whose pioneering book *The Spiral Dance* helped shape our circle's rituals, whose "Witch Camp" taught me to value the uniqueness of our own circle's celebrations. In Boulder, the mother I call to is rarely ancient—she's vital, strong, fertile. Is she thirty? Forty-five? As my mind hurried to the diversion of everyday tasks, I returned my awareness to the gentle rhythm of the chant, absorbing its reassuring repetition.

The Ancient Mother has no number, no age, just as a flower in bloom has no particular date—it is simply blossoming. Earth, the primordial mother, is at once fresh and primal, ancient and vital, pure and sensual, sad and loving.

The Ancient Mother of the Australian rocks is different, just as the earth in Australia is different—quieter, more subdued. Connected to the oldest continent in the world, I began listening to its hushed whisperings. Outcroppings like Woolshed Falls are smooth and rounded, with none of the jagged abruptness of the Rockies, Earth's youngest upstart mountains.

■ ■ ■

In the heart of Australia's red desert, Ayers Rock, Uluru, once lay beneath an antediluvian ocean that, over eons filled and dried, filled and dried again, finally leaving the vast expansive Red Centre of rock and sand. Ages and ages of water and wind stripped away the surrounding sand, leaving Uluru in polished, solitary magnificence, revealed as one of Earth's largest monoliths, keeping countless stories and songs locked within.

Perhaps part of my task is simply dancing with the dualities, moving from out-breath to in-breath, from youngest to oldest, from energetic to quiet—just as my dreams continue their daily—or nightly—soul working, whether I notice them or not.

Slowly, I began creating altars, reminders of the four directions, guardians of the elements of earth, air, water, and fire, re-creating a continuing circle in my Finch Street nest.

The casual eye would hardly have recognized my simple collection of treasures for the meaningful altars they were for me. A huge Australian pinecone held a jaunty collection of feathers on the living room mantle, flanked by poems from Doris and Barbara—one poem became a symbolic sentinel of the East, of dawn and new beginnings, and the other watched over the West, where the sun sets, a guardian of endings, closure and completion.

In the North, the smiling faces of the women's group, arranged in a mandala, marked the direction of Earth, for the grounding they give me. The collages they sent me provided lighthearted splashes of color above my writing table; their deep, fluid richness seemed to suit the watery West.

When I first began my soul work in women's circles, it took more than a year before I could fully face the North with its primal Earth mysteries. A mystery holds more meaning than I could comprehend. And since my upside-down year had barely begun, the South had no altar but remained open, as haunting and deeply mysterious as the North first had been to me.

With the circle completed, the directions marked, it was safe for me to open up to whatever might be—even a place where the burning sun comes from the North and storms and harsh winds from the South.

■ ■ ■

The next day, as I wandered through one of Beechworth's import galleries, an Indian weaving caught my eye and I decided to splurge on it to celebrate feeling reconnected to the circle. Leaving with my parcel, I noticed the shop's name: "Don't Panic." According to the *Hitchhiker's Guide to the Galaxy*, "Don't Panic" was one of the Universe's important messages—one that continually popped up in the most unlikely, incongruous settings. As the name of a small shop on Ford Street, the reminder not to panic struck me as a bit of serendipity, another nudge to remind me to share a smile with the powers of creation. No way to tell if the message came from the almost-forgotten book or from the cosmos. Or both.

I decided to thank the cosmos.

With child-like circles of tulips and scallops in crayon shades of honey brown, pink, and green, the Indian spread covered my bed; a center mandala of daisies added to its femaleness, offering a simple, visual reminder of the circle's soft embrace that covered me as I dreamed.

Dreaming, yes, but not thinking. Why hadn't I realized that my adventure down under also meant a year living outside the circle? The circle's weekly gatherings, the group's excitement at creating rituals always renewed my awareness of the invisible ebb and flow of life. Recognizing the sacred in our own seemingly personal passages, we slowly cleared a way to see the larger significance, the core meaning, in the mess and muddle of our everyday lives. The absence of a circle of like-minded women left a looming empty space of unknown dimensions, its boundaries to be explored. My journey had made me into a solitary practitioner.

I returned to walking the hills of Beechworth. They were first called Mayday Hills, the name given a mental hospital that preceded the town by decades. The town's granite highlands have had a reputation as a healing place for a long time, though no one here knows exactly why.

Boulder, too, was something of a healing center, drawing Buddhists and body workers, shamen and scholars. Boulder is also known for its schemers and shams.

Beechworth seems too small for that, but it has its mysteries—its name, for example. There are no beech trees, nor is there a European counterpart for which Beechworth was named. One old story claims that an anxious, frightened Chinese miner ran here searching for a doctor when his wife was having difficulties in labor. He struggled to say "breech birth," and the doctor heard it as "Beechworth," a name that stuck to the mining settlement.

It's as good an explanation as any.

■ ■ ■

The jingle of the postman's bicycle bell startled me from my reverie as I walked along the footpath. The postie nodded and I smiled, amused by his perpetual frown—an odd way to preserve his dignity as he biked along the path, a sprightly basket of mail perched on the handlebars, surprising those who got in his way with a cheery, childish tinkle.

Perfect timing. I found he'd left a letter from Barbara that, evoking an ancient Celtic blessing, asked if the ground had come up to meet me.

It had. Nearly every walk yielded some special gift, some treasure that appeared at my feet. Red, blue, and green feathers brightly proclaiming joyful abandon; crisp black and white magpie feathers that offered studies in the beauty of clear boundaries. A tree root evoking the magic Egyptian eye that surveys all creation. The tiny jawbone of a rabbit and the iridescent shell of a green Christmas beetle spoke to me of the beauty that lingers long after life departs.

Like magic crumbs, they urged me along the path leading deeper into the enchanted forest. Slowly I learned to open to their lessons. Bit by bit, the tiny natural treasures began to fill the emptiness of my flat. If I'd found such magical objects in Boulder, they would have seemed like clear signs of approval from Mother Earth.

"My problem is that I forget what I know," Grandma used to say.

Me, too.

It was a joy—and a relief—each time I remembered to "circle up" and join in the larger dance, knowing my hand was held, whether I could see the others in the circle or not.

CROSSING THE BOUNDARY RIVER

One bright autumn day in March, Robin proposed we venture to a new event, the Mind-Body Fair, something that promised to be unlike anything they'd ever seen in "the big smoke," the nearby towns of Albury-Wodonga. Their juxtaposed names evoked the genial incongruity I'd been growing accustomed to in Oz—much like exotic bottle brush trees blooming next to lilacs. The Murray River divided the two country towns as well as the states of Victoria and New South Wales, Robin explained as we drove over the low, smooth bridge.

The notion of a river as a boundary would seem odd to Koori people, however. A river is the unifier, the veins and arteries of a living system among people who define tribal lands by a whole river's drainage system. The rivers, the waters, are unifiers, while the subtle changes in topography and vegetation that mark the edges of watersheds are the lines that separate one group's land from another's.

But Albury-Wodonga had its own way of blurring boundary distinctions by sharing a railroad station, an airport, and a civic center that, as we approached, was being circled by a handful of placard-carrying protesters. Nearing the clutch of women circling the entrance to the low, blonde brick building, I was startled by the anger of one who insistently thrust a pamphlet into my hand. It protested the coming of the New Age to their sleepy, river-edge community. Their leaflet decried the New Age as a devil-inspired plot. How strange, I thought, to feel menaced by back-to-the-future vendors offering herbal cosmetics, crystal jewelry, and hand-painted silk bags. Merchant stalls lined the entry into a gym-like room. The heavy Andean wool sweaters and indigo-saturated garments of Guatemalan textiles seemed identical to those in countless festivals and craft fairs in Boulder; the aging hippies differed only in their accents while the flower children seemed a bit heartier. Festive but familiar offerings of ten-minute massages, reflexology or Reiki, sessions with Tarot readers, psychics, and numerologists lulled me into a comfort zone. Scanning the booths for something uniquely Australian, I was entranced by a brass bell encircled by light-catching amethyst chunks—just the feng shui touch to clarify your thinking when hung in your doorway. When you need a rationalization, any rationalization will do, I mused, succumbing to the spell of spiritual materialism.

The centerpiece of the fair was a small village of hand-painted tepees that filled the central courtyard. Nearby a local guru cited his California origins to hype tapes of his classes. Claiming the deep spiritual legacy of Tibet or Machu Picchu was one thing, but being a former resident of Los Angeles hardly seemed to qualify, I fumed, surprised at the anger and unexpected snobbishness this encounter triggered in me.

Continuing to search for any trace of the Koori who once walked this land, I found only a young man from Seattle named Kleinman who called himself Singing Wolf offering to tell Pacific Indian legends, and suddenly a clangor of internal voices began roaring: What is the force behind transforming Native American wisdom into a carnival sideshow and commercializing Native American spirituality? Can't they see the sacrilege inherent in degrading sacred objects into fashion trends? Even in small Australian country towns, the American twist on cultural imperialism—exporting its tackiest offerings—Coke and McDonalds, sitcoms and video violence—had elbowed aside the indigenous people of Australia for watered-down reflections of the people white America had nearly destroyed!

Shaking from a sense of violation, I couldn't listen to Kleinman–Singing Wolf's stories. Instead, I sat down to calm the churning mix of ownership and outrage, catch my breath, and tug the thread of memory. What emerged was a wispy glimpse of a ritual of childhood: going to Saturday matinees. Claiming a crusty, maroon velour seat in the popcorn-perfumed dark of the Fox Theater, I spent countless hours watching Westerns—and grieving for the Indians. The injustice of naming an enormous variety of tribes after an Italian explorer's mistake made me want to weep. Calling men "braves" or "chiefs," the women "squaws" filled me with indignation, walling me off from other Colorado six-year-olds.

The over-ripe Technicolor images filled me with a wistful longing for strong tribal connections even as I fumed at a Hollywood that portrayed blue-eyed Indians. One nameless film leapt out, and I clearly remembered feeling the loss and pain as I watched one man solemnly paint his face with symbols of mourning. Then he crept into a tepee with murderous intent—as if he'd donned war paint! Filled with fury at whoever could not read the signs of deep loss, I mourned portraying the Sioux as villains, the Comanche as bloodthirsty barbarians. Although I didn't know the word "racism" nor understand stereotypes, I sensed that something more malevolent than ignorance lay behind the errors and misrepresentations gleaming in mythic dimensions on the movie screens. Silently, I disavowed my culture's message that

Native Americans were bad, ignorant savages; I rejected the notion that they sprang from cultures that deserved to be destroyed.

Gradually outgrowing matinees, I also put away the anger with no outlet, coating my outrage with layers of understanding, like an oyster smoothing the grit that would not go away. I was grown and a mother before someone explained soul prints—strong feelings for a particular place and time that could be memories left from a past life. Growing comfortable with shape-shifting dreams, I still claimed to be an agnostic about reincarnation and past lives, even while the soul print fragments rippled on the edge of recollection like a feather headdress ruffled by a breeze.

As past-life regressions became the flavor of the month and every third person in Boulder claimed an Indian spirit guide, my not-quite-recovered memories were too embarrassing to discuss. Back in the 1950s, my great uncle, Scotty, had an Indian spirit guide, one practical and personal enough to warn him that his tire was going flat as he and his wife sped across the Utah desert to visit us in Colorado. His guide appeared on the hood of his car, pointing to the tire, giving Scotty time to pull over and avoid a high-speed blowout.

How I yearned for guidance that clear. How handy to have a vision to alert me of impending disaster. But no such luck. Scotty had died before I knew to ask him what to do and, try though I might, I found no way to shape what danced below my consciousness into any sort of guide.

Instead, I'd suddenly find my heart racing as I drove across some new mountain pass, the hair on the back of my neck bristling. "Ute Country," I'd confide to the dashboard, giving voice to the unexpected terror. Cresting an unfamiliar rise in the road, I'd find myself scanning a crenellated, lichen-covered ridge and muttering "ambush rocks" without knowing where the words came from. Poignancy, somehow, was a signal of kinship, a faint pulse I followed through dream-hole dimensions to where I came to understand that some part of me had lived as a Plains Indian woman, not too long ago, not too far from my home in Boulder. Maybe the cloudy memories spared me from recalling every painful detail—until I stood in the Albury-Wodonga Civic Center, still awash in a flood of unexplored memories, thrust through a time-dimensional wormhole.

■ ■ ■

Vowing to return and examine those memories when no New Age carnival beckoned, I sought something familiar—and preferably un-evocative. A workshop called "Harmonic Singing" seemed promising. When I'd taken part in Ysaye Barnwell's African American singing workshop, I'd seen the way close vocal harmonies had created a community of blacks and whites, Buddhists, and Christians and those who honored Oshun, Maat, and Isis. Thanks to Barnwell's full-throttle teaching, my bones had come to know the power of collective sound, my body the joy of stomping in joyful syncopation. Among joined voices and shared songs, I began to trust my own voice.

Expecting perhaps an a cappella group or a spontaneous chorus, I was puzzled to see only a bearded young man alone, center stage. How could he harmonize all by himself?

"There's nothing particularly magical about making harmonics," Andrew explained by way of introduction, "although the sounds may seem mystical or ethereal." Folding his lean limbs into a lotus position, he took a deep breath, closed his eyes, and began creating clear, flute-like notes that swelled and ebbed, sliding from bells to harp, then didgeridoos. A jubilation of bush birds warbled with the magpies, then the haunting calls of humpback whales filled the room as a bassoon-like drone held a silvery bottom note.

I was flabbergasted.

Opening his eyes, Andrew quietly explained that he'd been mesmerized when he first heard harmonics sung, and though he was a classically trained musician, couldn't figure it out. He began asking Australian musicians and was told that the ancient technique was first practiced by Mongolian horsemen who spent long evenings singing to the hills centuries ago; Tibetan monks later started practicing a variation called "throat singing" because it bypasses the vocal chords.

"But how do you do it?" Andrew asked in exasperation.

"I don't know," one of his mates responded, "but I'm sure it's dead easy." When it became clear he'd find no local tutors, Andrew set out to teach himself. Singing over the roar of waves crashing along the seashore, until he learned to sound two notes simultaneously, he then learned to control the harmonic sounds. "Once you have the trick, it's just a matter of practice," he said matter-of-factly, then produced a diaphanous version of "Amazing Grace." He would soon offer a workshop nearby and asked anyone interested to sign up for more information.

Reassured by his quiet capability—and an explanation free of New Age hokum—I decided that learning harmonic singing would be just the thing, a lovely piece of everyday magic to bring back to the women's circle. I hoped to give them a real taste of down-under enchantment, and what could be better than sounding like Australian birds?

How much his workshop would cost, where it would be, or how I could get there seemed minor concerns. I asked the fates to help make it happen. Floating on otherworldly sounds, heart wide open to a universe of new possibilities, I returned to the hubbub of fair-goers to look for Robin.

"Aura portraits," Robin said, pointing to a Polaroid picture taped to her shirt. The woman who interpreted her aura had reported intimate details of Robin's life, showing more than common insight. "You really should give it a go," she bubbled.

In full harmonic afterglow, I inhaled her enthusiasm and joined the lengthening queue for an aura portrait and couldn't avoid the man barking out pseudo-scientific details explaining how electrical impulses from your hand were transformed into an aura image that, not magically, mind you, but scientifically, registered on Polaroid film. Before my skepticism made its way to the surface, he peeled away a photo of my somewhat dazed face smiling slightly, head enveloped by a blue-green cloud. Somehow the photo reflected just the way I felt; I shuffled forward to have Elizabeth read my newly revealed fuzzy green aura.

With lanky, blonde-brown hair, Elizabeth looked like an Australian housewife in her late fifties. Taking my photo in her hand, she gazed at me and said my aura indicated I'd made many significant changes in my life—and the changes were not yet finished. Her genuine concern brought tears to my eyes as a wave of oceanic compassion hit me like a tsunami. She smiled and glanced at the little photo again.

"You've come into this life on the green ray, the heart ray, which means you must follow your feelings. Not reason or logic, even though they have a strong pull for you," Elizabeth said.

More tears arose from a bottomless sense of loss.

"Hope is what has been lost," she continued, nodding to acknowledge my tears, "and with it a sense of trusting that the world is safe." I saw silver-blue dreams entwined with green tendrils of hope that were mysteriously torn away, then trampled into red-brown dust. Crystalline blooms of promise burst open, then smashed into shards. I struggled to breathe as the sharp cascading cycles of numinous images rose and fell.

"Trust your feelings," Elizabeth urged.

Distrust was not the problem, it was the flash flood of feelings that shook me, the reawakened fears I'd learned too well. Vulnerable, yes, fine. But I floundered, near drowning, in oceanic swells of feeling.

As Elizabeth murmured reassurances, I glimpsed my usual strategy—a possum, shutting down, trying to breathe almost imperceptibly, a response every cell in my body knew. Wordlessly, she encouraged me to go deeper, look further. The energy of the wombat came, urging me to dig, to root out the source.

If you're going to fall, then jump; it's a lesson I learned as a child. When dream monsters chased me to the edge of a cliff, I discovered that if I jumped, I could bounce. Once I remembered, I could gather the courage to leap off, feel a scary and reassuring thunk, and then trampoline high up into the air. Knotted with fear, I'd bounce once, twice, three times, each bounce slowing. With each bounce, I'd grow more calm, reminding myself that, in the dreamworld, I could choose. Sometimes, I could remember in the middle of a fall. Remembering to choose the jump would transform the stomach-in-the-solar-plexus terror into resignation. The trampoline bounces themselves weren't exciting; the thrill came from knowing they'd slowly diminish. Remembering that I could endure smaller and smaller bounces until they stopped, I could finally walk away from the cliff, foiling whatever monsters pursued me. Decades later, I learned this response was a form of conscious dreaming.

First touchstone with ordinary reality, to see what had recently entered my consciousness: Quinn, Tia, and I had just seen the provocative film *JFK*, which reawakened a long-suppressed sense of loss I shared with a whole generation. We all remember where we were the moment we heard President

Kennedy had been shot. I remember sitting in the pediatrician's office, holding my month-old daughter, Catlyn. But for me the loss entwined with a nameless fear. We were living in Shreveport, where people called Kennedy a traitor. Where each night the television stations signed off with pictures of darkies picking cotton as the strains of "Dixie" rose to a stirring crescendo.

How did I wind up in Shreveport, a place that opposed everything I valued? That hid its dark love of violence beneath clouds of azaleas and drawled offerings of sweetened iced tea? The assassination of a president—unthinkable a moment before—shattered our whole nation's sense of safety, not just my own.

A wave of assassinations—Bobby Kennedy, Martin Luther King, Jr., and Malcom X—wrote the same bloody message: All the good men, the brave and heartful leaders, will be murdered. Those who managed to survive lived surrounded by assassins. That threat became personal, mingling with the violence I'd felt; betrayals hardened like cement around my ankles, a weight of hopelessness pulling me down further.

Shreveport's hidden forces drew a poisonous strength from the assassinations, something that occasionally slithered out above the surface, leaving the scent of threat hanging in the air. It clung to my skin, clogged my throat, fed a heart-pounding fear that sounded as soon as I took a few tentative steps toward activism, working on political campaigns, exercising the independence I had assumed was mine. Unexplained actions filled me with dread; I felt like I'd glimpsed hooded cobras out from the corner of my eye, snakes that disappeared as I turned to look at them directly: A car followed me and forced me off a deserted country road. Because I was the Yankee outsider? The phone rang, someone breathed heavily, said nothing, hung up. I felt the silent hatred of the unspoken message. When I awoke to ominous heaps of Klan flyers stuffed between the screen and the front door, I knew they'd found me. A cross burning on the quiet suburban lawn firmly tamped my idealism. Moving away, I became Possum woman, then gave birth to a second daughter. I reeled in recollection, swam against the tides of time, struggling to regain my place in the everyday world, out of the quicksand past.

"Heartfulness," Elizabeth said, her words pulling me back from the hole in space and time. I caught a glimpse of the booth at the Mind-Body Fair, even as my mind spun backward, reviewing my self, my life in strobe shots of clarity.

My inventory of internal resources tends to over-value thinking, I realized, as scene after scene appeared as if on a screen inside my head. Remembering that brought a sigh of relief. Listing and sorting were like clicking through my worry beads, bringing image after memory to calm me. But heartfulness wasn't on my rosary. What could I do with heartfulness? I panicked. Could I simply remember my heart? Would that keep it open?

"That means with tears streaming down your face," said a snide internal voice. "Not very attractive." Attractive? What have I been attracting? That question aroused a new, more gentle voice. "I've used time, often to my benefit. Now time is using me." I breathed into the new realization: Now was the time for my open, aching heart simply to be. Its openness, my openness, was all that was needed. I didn't have to figure it out. I didn't have to name the cobras or embrace the fear or understand the terror that shrouded hatred kindled inside me. I could simply be—filled with all the complexities and questions and confusion.

"Heartfulness," she repeated, as if presenting me with the key to everything. "You understand with your heart." Clinging to Elizabeth's shoulders as sobs as strong as birth pangs shook my body, I slowly surfaced. Her crooning soothed me back into an awareness of my surroundings, of other fair-goers impatiently waiting to have their aura portraits read.

"You are not only fine, but heartful," Elizabeth said reassuringly, offering a tissue as I blotted my streaming eyes and wiped my running nose. "Don't be afraid. Those are growing pains," she crooned. "You can be glad. You're not trapped by bitterness or sadness."

A flood of tears—even embarrassingly public ones—seemed a small price to pay for the key she had, in fact, given me. I began opening the door to understanding not with my head, not with my mind and its swarming memories, but with my heart.

I knew I had to find Robin.

Walking through the fair looking for her, I noticed that most of the other aura pictures taped on other people's shirts showed red, orange, or yellow, a few were pale whitish gray. I smiled. There wasn't another green-blue one in sight.

We found an oasis of plastic chairs and sofas and sat down with our paper cups of tea, eager to share what we'd experienced and wondering if we'd had enough of the Mind-Body Fair. We'd exchanged only glances when a man pulled away from the crowd and hailed Robin. "No time to duck him. I've been spotted," she whispered as he rushed over, brandishing some cards and insisted we both take the Luscher Color Preference Test right then and there. Elizabeth had given me enough to ponder, but Nigel would not be denied. We were cornered.

Listlessly, I chose.

Looking at the color cards I'd selected, then the aura picture still taped to my shirt, Nigel exclaimed over their "spot on" similarities. Both revealed love and heartfulness, he declared as I tried shrugging off his unwanted attention. And both indicated my loving personality, although my loving wasn't always right, or enduring, or reciprocated.

Reciprocated. Enduring. Love always included those words, I realized. Swallowing hard, I fought the tears that threatened to return. Crying with Elizabeth had been safe, but crying with Nigel was not. My heart knew.

Robin and I exchanged a glance of mutual relief as Nigel spied someone else on whom to spring his test. "He's an odd duck I've known casually for years. He enjoys showing off his psychological insight and I guess wearing our aura portraits just gave him another dimension to pounce on," Robin said. "His life's mission seems to be belaboring the obvious—just in case we didn't get it," she added with a conspiratorial grin. We headed back to Beechworth.

That night I dreamed a mysterious man was making love to me, sweetly trying to please me, although others tried to interrupt us. Warm with dreamy liquid pleasure, I awoke to realize how much I'd withdrawn from my body, shutting off the feelings, even closing off the delicate messages of every nerve ending, like slamming the lid of an old trunk. But that trunk was my torso. I began tentatively prodding my midsection which felt as rigid and stuffed as a sausage—and about as dead. Now, why haven't I let myself feel my body? The easy message of the dream is to blame all the months without a lover.

■ ■ ■

Perhaps I've always given lovers some special power, one that helps me to appreciate my own body. A lover's attention revitalizes the nuances of sensation. With no lover to reflect my physical vitality, I lazily retreat to the possum-like existence in my head, where my consciousness hovers like a helium balloon lightly tethered to my body.

Suddenly I was overwhelmed with a physical memory of my last lover, left behind in Boulder. Missing Matt also meant missing the awakening tingle of his hair brushing my skin into life, missing the soft, woody scent of his body, missing the way its gentle, funny shapelessness evoked a sad tenderness. Neglected, puffy, and over-full, my body felt as huge and blob-like as Matt's.

Now there's an odd memorial to a lost love!

Startled, I vowed to reawaken my body, not quite sure how to do that. Was there a way to remove all the energetic rocks that had fallen along my inside neural passageways, to reclaim the secret connecting tunnels where the walls have caved in, fallen down, and blocked the way from one chakra to the next? I began warming to the idea of a sort of internal reclamation project, then slowly realized how alien such an idea would be to a Koori woman. They don't distinguish between inside and out, waking and dreaming, the physical and the imaginal world. What would it be like to know my bones and the rock beneath my feet are the same, that what I know and what the wombat feels are the same? That listening with my feet is the same as dancing, that moving my body means talking with every cell of my being?

While a Koori's gliding, multi-dimensional awareness eluded me, I managed to recall that, in Boulder, I stretched every day and danced and moved each week, but I hadn't been doing any moving or dancing across Wimslow's concrete floor. Daily piddling bits of housework—flatwork—were the only breaks from writing, walking my only exercise, and somehow that was just moving my legs and arms, not my center.

A million romantic songs notwithstanding, listening inside reveals that there is so much more to listen to besides your heart. Can I simply be with that place inside and connect the threads of feelings? Touching that place brings only tears—although most of them are tears of recognition, not tears of sadness.

Perhaps the memories of Matt still saddened me, although he'd been gone nearly a year. More than simply the latest man to walk away, he was unique among all my lost lovers, because he helped me to love and appreciate myself. He took part willingly, often joyfully, in every co-ed ritual and improvisational dance, sharing the wacky creative chaos that fed me. When I decided to shed my father's name and my married name and celebrate the change with a renaming ritual, Matt wondered if it was appropriate for him, a relative new-comer in my life, to participate.

"You were sharing the kind of insights that people spent years in analysis to achieve," he said afterward. He was impressed by my courage, my willingness to speak inner secrets out loud; the mixture of pride and astonishment in his voice, his willingness to witness all that psychic skin-shedding touched me. Instinctively recognizing the importance of shar-ing these moments within the ritual circle, he didn't draw away from the open intimacy or trivialize the meaning that my handcrafted ritual held for me.

He was my Gemini twin, born just twenty-four hours before me, offering me twin-like reflecting that helped me stay in touch with my feelings and, perhaps, expand this growing heartfulness. Missing and mourning his twin-ness, I remembered Joel saying that twins were considered bad luck.

Twins born to a Koori woman could spell tragedy for the whole clan. When a woman has twins, the clan loses the hands of a gatherer and gains another mouth to feed, which can strain the people's resources beyond the breaking point.

Back in my Beechworth flat, a vase of wilted dahlias from the garden asked to be thrown out.

Tears always make my nose run, threatening to clog my breath, but I pushed beyond the distractions of each day's wilted dahlias and my reluctance to follow where tears took me. I'm too skilled at swallowing tears. I felt I'd spent a lifetime mastering how to stifle them.

"Time to go with the flow," I said, smiling as the cliché twisted from river to runny nose.

The Path to Weerona

mid the audience gathered for harmonic singing at the Mind-Body Fair, one woman had stood out—tall, generously proportioned, blond hair pulled back in an off-center braid that sprang from the side of her head. I felt instantly drawn to Jilba—perhaps because her energy reminded me of my friend Jennifer, whom I often found gardening in a paint-splattered sweatshirt, dirt-encrusted feet in dime-store rubber thongs—with kohl-rimmed eyes. I wondered how to get to know her, when good old fate intervened. Andrew, the instructor, ended his session at the Mind-Body Fair by announcing that he'd be teaching a weekend-long harmonic singing workshop that would be hosted by Jilba. That fascinating woman lived at a retreat center called Weerona somewhere in the upper Murray River valley. I only vaguely knew that was south and east of Beechworth, but it all felt so serendipitous that I decided to go, even if that meant hitching a ride a couple of weeks in the future.

Excited but transportation-challenged, I arranged a ride with the only two people certain to attend the workshop: Jilba and Andrew. They didn't appear to regard my asking as an imposition.

A few weeks later we met in Wangaratta for the drive. Climbing into a jeep, Jilba explained that a whole group would be gathered at Weerona to observe the Equinox with a sweat lodge, since the harmonic singing weekend began on March 21.

"Are you right with that?" she asked.

"I've never done a sweat, although I'd definitely be open to a new way of marking the Equinox," I said, and began the increasingly familiar mental wrestling required to meld observing March 21 as the Spring Equinox with the down-under reality of approaching autumn. Chagrined at mentally skipping the earth holidays I'd been observing for years, I welcomed the chance to join a group celebrating the Equinox. But marking it with a Native American ritual I'd yet to experience seemed an odd choice. Already committed to the weekend trip, however, I decided that perhaps an Aussie version of a sweat lodge might simply be another surprise gift from the universe. Who was I to question that?

Preparing for the long drive, Andrew and Jilba had stopped for a pizza, sharing their food back and forth like old friends. Sitting in the back, trying not to feel like the prover-bial odd woman out, I began puzzling about what this ritual might mean to them. First Jilba spoke of "looking forward to the sweat" in a way that sounded as mundane and secular as anticipating a soak in a hot tub, then veered off to the impor-tance of being cleansed before embracing harmonic singing. Andrew spoke so quietly that I struggled to hear his part of their conversation. Participating without shouting proved impossible.

Andrew put on a tape of some fourteenth century music that blanketed the possibility of any further talk, and I relaxed into an isolated sound capsule skimming along the moonlit countryside to weigh the prospects of a sweat lodge. Although I knew little about it, I had an almost reflexive respect for the ancient Lakota ritual, yet I'd held back from the opportunities to participate, shying away from the weekend warriors who offered random sweat lodge experiences as a key toward personal growth. How had a trendy Native American tradition made it all the way here, into rural Australia, I wondered again as fingers of mist grasped at the edge of the road. The winding, foggy moonlight drive next to the dammed-up strength of the Murray River seemed a perfect prelude to this journey into the unfamiliar.

Suddenly, responding to a silent, secret signal, Jilba slammed on the brakes and swerved sharply to the edge of the road. Before the jeep came to a full stop, she leaped out the door, grabbing a package of tobacco from the dashboard. I watched in astonishment as she stood, arms upraised to the sky, silently offering prayers and bits of tobacco to the four directions, honoring the spirit of the possum killed along the side of the road in classic Native American fashion. "That's just something I do—to make up for the road built through their land, for damming the river and changing their world," she said, hopping back in. I began to relax about the authenticity of the impending sweat lodge and instead began puzzling about how all this fit into Jilba's life.

A large, smashed water bird prompted a second abrupt stop, but this time, after saying her prayers and offering her blessings, Jilba suddenly grabbed the bird's wing and wrenched it violently, returning to the jeep with a large bunch of wing feathers. The feathers were to take home to Dan, so he could identify the bird and put its feathers to use, she explained.

After jouncing through the spooky, stubbled remains of a slashed forest, we passed through a series of gates, then drove alongside a meadow where four giant tepees gleamed like startling moonlight apparitions. On the front porch, the group ignored a "Shoes off, Please" sign as we made our way to the kitchen-dining-lounge room, the heart of Weerona's main house, arriving just as a ragtag group of people entered from the opposite direction. One young man wore a sheepskin coat over a towel and shoes, others clutched sarongs; all were dripping wet.

As we exchanged greetings, I pondered the room plastered with a Jennifer-esque assortment of dried flowers, crockery, pictures, antique tins, photos, and artfully arranged what-have-yous. Only when I saw an imposing oil portrait of Dan did I recognize him from the exhibition of tepees at the Mind-Body Fair. It was his collection of tepees that we had just passed in the meadow.

We newcomers were casually introduced to Jilba's Grandma, His-and-Hers teenagers, and her thirty-ish brother, Leon. A swarm of others idled about, making tea, rolling cigarettes, or watching the TV in the corner. We weren't introduced. Jilba commanded someone to turn off the TV; it created the wrong environment for those just emerging from the sweat lodge. The damp and dripping group had arrived earlier and had just finished their Autumnal Equinox sweat. A few other stragglers who hadn't made it in time for the first sweat were to join me, Andrew, and Jilba for a second round.

A basket in the laundry-shower room overflowed with sarongs—lighter than beach towels, these ubiquitous whiffs of cotton were unisex reminders that the tropical Pacific Islands are Australia's nearest neighbors. Handing me a sarong, Jilba pointed me to another room to change. Her bedroom proved to be another eclectic marvel: a cluster of glow-in-the-dark stars danced over an unmade bed. A stunning photo of a nude Jilba, seated, head bowed, looking perfectly Goddess-like adorned the table.

Unclear how undressed to get, I stripped and wrapped myself in a sarong, returned to the kitchen, then decided it might be wise to retrieve my shoes, in case the path were rocky. In a handkerchief-weight sarong and running shoes, not quite naked in front of the room full of strangers, I shifted from one foot to the other both mentally and physically as I waited.

Swathed in a black flowered sarong, this one elasticized at the top, Jilba reappeared and announced to Dan that, even though I'd come all the way from America, this was my first sweat lodge. This revelation prompted the slightly spaced-out company assembled to some good-natured joshing about having to travel around the world to learn about what I'd left behind. Then Jilba picked up a didgeridoo and commanded us into the moonlit darkness, leading the way along an invisible path to where a fire roared in front of the low, round sweat lodge. Once we all arrived, Dan smudged us from head to toe with burning sage, one by one, paying special attention to the soles of our now-bare feet. He instructed us to crawl into the waist-high structure one at a time, preceded by a Sioux prayer, or dedication, something that sounded like "Ho Wanne Tanka," which, he explained, meant, "For All My Family."

Clambering through the entry hole, I managed to keep wearing most of the sarong and was greeted by an intense, almost tangible, wall of heat. Squishing through the mud underfoot, I took my place in the circle next to Jilba, thankfully some distance from a young man named Frederick who smelled fiercely even before beginning the sweat. Seated next to the flap covering the entrance sat Dan, serving as a sort of master of ceremonies. In the center, a heap of rocks radiated energy. Ceremoniously, Dan called out to a fire keeper to bring in a rock; a pitchfork appeared with first one glowing, red-hot stone, then another. When six had been added, Dan hailed these new glowing presences as the rock people; their organic scarlet shapes radiated with the intensity of superheated volcanic lava. When someone murmured about spirit rocks, I knew I'd never before experienced rocks with such a stunning, solemn presence. The ember-like rocks firmed my resolve. All my misgivings fell quiet; I could fully experience my first sweat lodge.

Dan poured water on the rock people, releasing a hissing cloud of steam that left a dark, wound-like stain on each glowing rock. The prayers were to go around the circle moving from his right, on the topic of why we were grateful for our families, he explained. Anyone could choose to be silent, but we needed to mark the end of our turn, silent or otherwise, by saying "Ho" or "Ho He Wane Tanka." Jilba began playing the didgeridoo, its throbbing, insistent sound expanding the crowded sweat lodge like a balloon. Anchored with the smell of wet rock and mud under my body I relaxed into the hypnotic hum and prepared for the ritual's magic to unfold.

Dan's prayers were quite poetic, Jilba's heartfelt, and although major muddles surrounded my family connections, I managed to speak sincerely, not about my own family but of the next level of families and the net of Spider Mother that connects us all. To punctuate the end of each prayer, Dan splashed more water on the rocks, producing a dramatic hiss of steam and occasionally releasing a surprising whiff of sweet grass smoke as well. But as the prayers moved around the circle, I grew impatient as they began to seem trivial, hopelessly wordy, unfocused, and not well thought out: "Oh, dear Grandfathers, I just have so much to be grateful for," blah blah, blah. "Make me pure, make me worthy. I am so insignificant," blah, blah, blah. Rather than speaking from their hearts, most participants seemed to be playing to their audience and trying to impress Jilba and Dan with their piety.

After going full circle, Jilba led off a familiar chant: "Mother, I feel you under my feet. Mother, I feel your heart beat." Maybe because of the heat, maybe the late hour, but I felt little joy or energy—and then chastised myself for being so judgmental. Someone listlessly shook a rattle and began the second round of prayers. We were supposed to focus on the plant and animal world, with special attention to our animal teachers and helpers, Dan said, and just maybe ask for something for ourselves—which confirmed my sense that the prayers had been listless while also making me feel a bit scolded, as if I'd done it wrong the first round. A sheet of sweat covered me, my hair was hot to the touch, and the discomfort of sitting with my back unsupported expanded to a full-blown pain. How long was I going to have to endure? How could I keep from passing out from the heat? Again I tried focusing on the prayers, but they still seemed wordy, diffuse, and empty.

Suddenly I realized that a sweat lodge was a ritual about mortifying the flesh. It was part of the legacy of a people who responded to white oppression by shredding their bodies in the Sundance, priding themselves on the blood shed and proudly displaying their scars. What would happen if I were to flee? To flunk my first sweat lodge? My panic started rising with each new infusion of steam until another woman declared she needed a break. Several of us, Andrew included, clambered out after her, breathlessly grateful for the cool night air. I relished the chilled grass beneath my toes, marveled how the fire kept the mosquitoes away, and drank in the moonlight. When we were called back in, Andrew chose to stay outside. He didn't have to prove he was an American who could take it.

But refreshed enough to renew my stubborn determination, I re-entered the steamy dark. People didn't usually leave the lodge at the break between prayers, Jilba said to those who'd bolted. "It wasn't only me," I wanted to cry. "Others wanted to leave, too. And they didn't come back." But slowly I realized she wasn't scolding me, only trying to preserve the integrity of the ritual. Taking a deep breath, I tried to focus on the third round. Luckily, since the circle had shrunk, the prayers went more quickly—but with seemingly less meaning. Try though I might, I couldn't figure out the topic or even remember if Dan announced one.

Struggling with wobbling confusion and mildly bubbling paranoia, not to mention the physical discomforts, my mind scurried from one form of spiritual practice to another, recalling countless conversations: Debbie saying that during meditation your body can provide endless distractions. Peggy observing how some paths to enlightenment focus on cleansing the body—whether with colonics or purification baths, or sweat lodges; others, like meditation, try to transcend the body's existence, ignoring or abhorring the fact that we are embodied beings. And zealots who see suffering itself as the path to enlightenment—the way of the martyrs and the Penitentes. What a relief that my spiritual path didn't demand suffering or see the body as a mere container for a trapped or troubled soul.

Spaced out and sputtering, my steaming brain refused to connect my current misery with any enlightenment or hunt further for any other notion, spiritual or otherwise. So, short of bolting for the door, what could my body do? The rock on which I sat felt wonderfully cool. Placing my palms down, I tried to draw the rock's coolness inward. It didn't work. I remembered my initiation at Lake Steam Baths where a venerable attendant said your body's thermostat is at the back of your neck—which was why you hung a cool towel around your neck. I struggled to cool the back of my neck—to no avail. My fingers crept backward until I touched a hint of cool outside air. I tried to draw the cool upward from my fingertips. Another unsuccessful struggle. A drink of water didn't cool from the inside out. Finally, as the circle completed another round of prayers, I knew I couldn't face one more rock coming in the door. My body at overwhelm, I gave up and asked to leave the sweat lodge.

Outside, I opened myself to the near full moon, soaking in its lemon light like sipping a long, refreshing drink. Next to the fire Andrew waited for me, a towel tossed over his shoulders. Tightening my flimsy sarong more for modesty than warmth, I sat next to him, facing the fire. Two fully clad fire keepers kept their distance. I marveled that one felt cool enough to zip up his plaid flannel jacket, when my body radiated heat. A few yards from the fire, the farm's dam glinted a dark promise of water in the moonlight. Someone straggling out of the sweat lodge said you were supposed to jump into the water after leaving, but, grateful that my contrary judgmentalness was melting away, I didn't want to risk encountering any more "shoulds."

Andrew suggested we go inside and take a shower ahead of the others. He offered a couple of foam mattresses in his truck if I wanted one to make sleeping in the tepee more comfortable, and I realized that the tepees were our sleeping accommodations. Muffled singing and prayers still came from the sweat lodge, and, though drained, some part of me still longed to see the end of the ritual. As the last holdouts finally emerged, some threw themselves down on the grass—wish I'd thought of that when I was still so hot—while others jumped into the water, inhaling sharply, shrieking at the cold.

Black dirt streaked my legs, arms, and bottom. Did I look radiant, like the time last year when I'd painted my face with rich black dirt in a medicine wheel? Or was I simply grubby from hours of sitting in mud?

"Let's take that shower now, and maybe we can avoid a lineup," I said, heading along the path to the house.

A clear curtain emblazoned with multi-colored parrots defined the shower in a corner of the laundry-pantry-mud room. Andrew asked if I were cold or if I minded if he took the first shower. Go ahead, I motioned, still half-dazed, the sweat lodge heat still numbing my mind. Through the curtain, I stared at his lean, naked body. Don't gawk, I scolded myself, glancing around at the pantry shelves lined with jeweled jars of sliced pears and peaches.

"Canning is almost a lost art," I offered, groping for a neutral topic.

"Not in the country," he replied, halting the only conversational foray I could muster. I returned to staring at Andrew's smooth, glowing, nearly incandescent body.

When it was my turn to shower, I realized I'd forgotten a towel. No way the mud-smeared sari would suffice. Andrew handed me his and offered to wait and help me get settled in one of the tepees.

He produced a pair of the twin-bed-sized foam mattress pads that every rural Aussie seems to own. Placing them along the south side of the tepee, I unrolled my borrowed sleeping bag, which proved impossible to rezip in the darkness. Still carrying the warmth of the sweat lodge, I felt no chill, just a wave of relief: At last I knew that the sweat lodge was not my ritual. For years, I'd never felt called to it, found reasons not to go when an opportunity arose, but I'd never known why. The sweat lodge didn't belong to me, I realized, indulging in the special, secret thrill that comes when my own experience confirms some irrational prejudice.

Andrew threw a precautionary blanket over our feet, then suddenly turned to me with a rather startling question, "What do you think about men, in general?"

"I don't much care for men, in general," I replied, surprising myself by blurting out the truth. "Men, in general, men, as a group, seem alarming," I explained. "They start wars and dig up the insides of Mother Earth. They burn and scrape off her vegetation to plant what they choose. They dam her rivers, pollute her oceans, and seem to have almost no regard for other creatures living on this planet.

"But," I said, slowly realizing the negativity of my words, "some men in particular, some individuals, like my brother, Quinn, or my friend Paul, are men I love dearly. Some, like the men offering prayers tonight, give me hope for a growing new —or perhaps very ancient—awareness of our connections to each other and to the earth."

Before Andrew had a chance to respond to my mini sermon, someone stuck a head into our tepee scouting out a space for Sue to sleep. "No worries," he said, moving my mattress closer to his, a move that made room—and a momentary awkwardness. We'd be sleeping right next to each other—and darned if I could puzzle out the social, cultural, or sexual expectations of this situation.

Luckily Sue, the unwitting chaperone, arrived, and the tepee became a shared space, like any summer camp. Gently spreading blankets over both of us, he whispered goodnight, and I contemplated the silence, the pattern of moonlight dancing among the poles at the top of the tepee, the scent of the night air, and the way damp hair doubled my sense of coolness. Gazing at his moonlit profile as he lay sleeping—or pretending to—I asked myself if I were turned on by this gentle poet-musician. It was a relief to find no internal electrically charged twinges. Safe from any wild surges mounting a sneak attack on my decision, I relaxed, recalling the loving, but brotherly touches, the caring closeness I'd felt with other men, like Paul. The unfamiliar but comforting sound of snuffling horses outside the tepee lulled me to sleep as it neared 3 a.m.

When the kookaburras and magpies sang the dawn's arrival, a campfire was already lit in the center of the circle of tepees. Several people I recognized from last night's sweat lodge wandered about making tea and munching breakfast. Not awake enough to crash a circle of people who already knew each other—and uncertain about waiting for Andrew—I strolled up to the main house by myself.

Reaching the top of a small rise, I gazed back to the tepees wrapped in a scarf of early dawn haze. Untethered horses stirred in the fog-filled meadow as they grazed in a tiny dream-like village, and I fell back in time, to living on the Great Plains in a seemingly endless series of tranquil days that each dawned with rich possibilities. Wherever that memory sprang from, in whatever past life, I re-experienced a soft, golden time as a Plains Indian, living with no fear, no tension, no threat of war, hostility, or destruction. I basked in an unfamiliar sense of being gently held by that small community as if cradled in milkweed silk, the smell of summer grass, the whir of grasshoppers, the lassitude of a mildly dawning summer sun. Breathing a silent prayer of thanks for being able to bring that strong, peaceful recollection to this lifetime, I thought that perhaps reconnecting with that distant memory of quiet joy might be the whole reason for my trip.

Still feeling meditative, I strolled through the empty veranda into a kitchen overflowing with the bustle of family and visitors departing, the smell of tea and toast, the gentle clatter of spoons and bowls and cups. Viva arrived first, a smiling, vibrant woman who, I guessed, had seen more than seventy summers. She and I had connected briefly at the Mind-Body Fair where Andrew was demonstrating harmonic singing. Hearing my name, Viva introduced herself; my name had been her maiden name and she was tickled to hear it spoken.

Olwyn, Sue, and Wendy emerged from the tepees and Peter, a total newcomer, drove up in his ute (his truck).

Addressing the small group lounging on the grass, Andrew said that the terms "harmonic singing," or "throat singing" are misleading names, since the sounds have nothing to do with the voice: Harmonics are overtones that have both a mathematical and a musical relationship to the fundamental note. Overtones are always present, though not always easy to hear. In singing, the fundamental note sounds like a steady drone while the overtones of that note float above the base sound. He diagrammed the patterns of sound waves and demonstrated a harmonic series with a guitar string. A proven dunderhead who'd never learned how to read music, I was overwhelmed by the flood of technical details, hoping I'd have a chance to try doing it before I went under.

Your body contains a whole column of air and your diaphragm provides the "oomph" to push your breath upwards, he continued. Your throat, mouth, and tongue vary the size, shape, and, consequently, the acoustics of the sounding chamber. In essence, you don't sing but allow your body to become a musical instrument; the trick is getting your vocal cords out of the way and let the pure, ethereal harmonics emerge.

These sounds extend beyond our usual system of musical notation, he said, an idea that moved it into the realm of enchantment: The novel experience of listening for subtle harmonics emerging from a voice was like tuning into another dimension. I just knew those sounds were magic the first time I heard them.

Step One was learning to breathe like a musical instrument, trying with first one vowel sound then another. After a bit of practice, I could create some harmonics—sounds so soft and subtle that I couldn't tell how much resonated inside my head and how much others could hear. Having gone that far, I was torn between wanting to practice and being curious about the others' progress. When Andrew paired us off for more practice, I was partnered with Viva who declared she could hear my harmonics quite clearly—and then couldn't wait to move on to chatting with the others.

That evening, Jilba and Dan wanted to give the group an introduction to Native American culture and show us a video they treasured. Once a transient sheepshearer, Dan had his life transformed by studying with a Lakota teacher from Pine Ridge in the Dakotas. He learned to make traditional tepees and earned permission to lead sweat lodges. Committed to a life that drew heavily upon Native American spirituality, Jilba and Dan had a small business selling spiritual and Native American books, animal cards, and sage candles by mail order "because they're bloody hard to locate down here," he laughed.

"But what led you down this path? Why the fascination with things Indian?" I couldn't help asking. "Why approximate a Native American existence here?"

"We're all natives of this planet," he said, clearly fielding a familiar question. "My teacher is one of those who believes it's time to speak native teachings and share a sort of native attitude. Caring for the earth, conserving its resources, living gently on the planet—that's what's important. We all move about so much that it hardly matters where you were born."

The narrator of the BBC video spoke the words of long-dead Indians, recounting their views of the world while images of the Rocky Mountains, the Black Hills, and the Great Plains flashed on the screen. Old black-and-white portraits of Indian faces stared solemnly at us as the narrator explained that birds build round houses and the Indians build round tepees, which means birds and the tepee dwellers are of the same tribe—an intriguing, unfamiliar notion that I hadn't heard before. But an annoyingly loud, electronically sampled meadowlark call in the sound track confused me. I thought the filmmakers added the meadowlark's trill at wildly inappropriate times—like when the plains were gripped by winter snows—a clear indication that the essence of the relationship between the people and the birds had somehow escaped the filmmakers. I felt both smug and embarassed by my esoteric nitpicking.

Before our goodnights to Jilba and Dan, the singing students agreed to meet in silence in the main house kitchen at 6:30 in the morning to have a silent cup of tea, then take a meditative walk.

Andrew had been busy down by the tepees, building a fire and, to update our tiny tribal center, hauled out two super-sized stereo speakers and opened his CD collection. The darkening meadow grew rich with ethereal sounds: harmonic voices and world music in mysterious languages, strings, and gamelans, horns and doumbeks, and scads of other exotic instruments I could only admire, not name. We assumed the fire-tender roles as others joined the music fest, then drifted off to bed until only those of us from the singing workshop remained staring into the embers. Olwyn and Viva led off some Girl Guide campfire songs, introducing another persistent international culture: Olwyn, who'd grown up in London, knew all the same versions of the camp songs that Viva had learned in Australia more than thirty years earlier. The rest of us lent our voices, launching into unknown harmonies and stumbling over obscure lyrics and laughing our way through semi-familiar variations.

To reach beyond the scouts' cannon, I taught them "The River is Flowing."

"That's an Indian song," said Fay, breaking her long silence by singing a version that ended with a drum, drum, drum beat.

Olwyn and I simultaneously remembered the same version of "We All Come from the Goddess," and I wondered if these were now being sung around Global Goddess Scout campfires. Or perhaps we'd all become Hundredth Monkeys, tapping into a larger realm beyond personal knowing, like the English sparrows who all simultaneously learned how to take the tops off milk bottles, forcing dairies to redesign their bottle caps and rethink porch deliveries.

No Hundredth Monkey awareness, nor even simple memory, had touched me when it came to camping basics, however. I'd simply hurled myself into the experience, heeding only my excitement, it seemed. I was humbled by how utterly unprepared I was for a weekend of tepee living. Without a flashlight or some drinking water, I couldn't perform the simple bedtime task of brushing my teeth. Reluctant to request anything from Andrew and hoping a lighthearted tone would cover my embarrassment, I asked if he'd give me some of his water to brush my teeth if I promised to be ever so good.

"And just how good would that be?" he responded with a knowing smile—not the response I'd hoped for.

"I promise not to spit in your canteen," I said. My lame attempt at lightness instantly made me cringe. Handing me his canteen, he left to stow away his stereo equipment as I crawled into the tepee, grateful for the darkness that hid my embarrassment, and fell asleep.

We awoke together and wordlessly snuggled spoon fashion, listening as Sue slipped out quietly, watching the sun paint the horizon pink through the tepee's circular doorway. Curling into his body felt utterly comfortable—and confusing. I found myself responding to him as if we were lovers. Cuddles don't have to be sexual, I reminded myself. Awaking together to a bird-filled dawn, the fresh air and the sky can simply be a glorious human experience, I scolded as he drew me closer, involving my fingers in a playful experiment with the sense of touch. Stroking the back of my hand set off a gentle, full-body riffle, arousing a skin hunger that I'd struggled to forget. Gently caressing my breasts, he embraced the convexness of my stomach without sexual urgency; far more erotic than casual, his touches were still as ambiguous as my responses. Some not-yet-realized dread kept me from yielding to the moment—like trying to soak in a mountain hot spring while wondering when the armed and outraged property owner will appear—as his breath warmed the back of my neck, his feathery kisses dangerously close to a spot that always aroused my desire.

What was the stopper? What stood in the way?

A snide voice in my head replied: "You're being played for a fool. You're practically old enough to be his mother," damning us both with an icy splash. I recognized the voice that evoked every social convention and behavioral cliché—and instantly knew it was wrong. Am I quashing my own yearnings? Worried about what other people will think? Did Andrew expect something more from me because we shared a shower or slept snuggled together? Or had I, both flattered and puzzled, made too much of his attentions? None of those explanations rang true. All I got was a warning not to venture there—even if I couldn't find the reason.

If he has any expectations, he's certainly old enough to handle them, I decided, fleeing our shared sleeping bag still wrapped in warmth and closeness. Clutching the morning mist rich with dewy eucalyptus, I headed for the main house, determined to move toward a more contemplative, sacred space, struggling to focus on the walking dawn meditation, my mind still buzzing its honeybee direction dance.

Something else. Something about sleeping with the teacher, said each footfall. Something about how sex disrupts the powerful creative tension between teacher and student: Upsetting that sacred and time-honored pattern unleashes something dangerous and unpredictable. Like with Todd, who had been so gentle and appreciative when I was his student, a professor careless about his advantage. And I, living the archetype of young and foolish, trusted the power of following the path of breadcrumbs, the yellow brick road, and believed I could handle anything—including Shreveport, even though I'd never set foot south of the Mason-Dixon Line.

Figuring it out, at least that far, brought me a bit of relief, quieting the mind-buzz, giving me something like a reason to cling to.

In the kitchen, some nodded and smiled a welcome as they prepared their tea; Olwyn and Jilba seemed lost in an interior place. Others seemed as if they'd decided that silent equaled glum.

Just outside the windows, I felt the ghosts of Koori people gathering in the mist, a reminder that greeting one another with a smile isn't their way. There's no way to know if the person you encounter is dealing with loss or illness or some other sadness, so smiles are an unwelcome intrusion, they reason, and you can never know what a person has just experienced as you first encounter them.

One by one we moved outside, past the tennis court, slowly walking single file through a small gate by the bower bird tree. Try to stay aware of the earth moving up to meet each footstep, Jilba had suggested. I noticed my balance shift as my pace slowed and breathing in time with my steps focused new clarity on my surroundings: the dam smelling faintly of mud and reeds, the air cooler by the water's edge where a few duck feathers rocked in the shallows. My passing did not even stir them. Water gurgled into a shallow ravine, lush and cool, a small bridge of flat-topped stones spanned the overflow from a nearby spring, connecting the lush farm with uncultivated pasture. Beyond the green-splotched bridge, the carpet of grass gave way to earth as rocky, dry, and hardened underfoot as a Colorado prairie. In the spaces between tussocks of coarse grass, small dark rabbit droppings rolled like marbles beneath our feet.

A brown hawk soared in a lazy demonstration of the principles of gliding. The keerawongs, with their autumn call to "Chop, Chop, Chop, Wood," appeared to chase the hawk away. Overhead, the parrots, cockatoos, wagtails, and galahs swooped to catch an unperturbed breakfast; in our silence we had become part of the landscape.

Atop the hill, Jilba awaited us wrapped in a Peruvian poncho, a cross-cultural Goddess in sculptural splendor, a didgeridoo for her scepter. Out of courtesy or reflex, I followed her gaze to the surrounding foothills, half-cleared of timber, their thick skirts of smoky-green eucalyptus hemmed with the dark ruffles of pine plantations. Feeling the sun warming my back awake, I stretched into a lazy imitation of Olwyn's Tai Chi movements, enjoying the soft, quiet crunch of muscle and bone and sinew, stretching into the awareness that something inside me had shifted. More than a year before, after Matt left, I'd gracelessly stumbled into celibacy, rather than making a conscious choice. For most of my life, sex had been a delightful distraction, but celibacy had given me a deeply pleasurable connection with spirit. I hadn't been conscious of its subtle satisfaction until that moment.

Jilba's didgeridoo welcomed the sun and awakened the hills with rolling, throbbing sound, and I silently gave thanks. I felt liberated by knowing that, if another man came into my life, we would first connect on another level besides the sexual, however sweet that could be.

Wordlessly, our small group gathered in a circle and seemed to become didgeridoos ourselves, releasing sounds that slowly swelled into rich harmonics that soared into the morning sky. As the clear notes climbed, Andrew's eyes smiled at mine, warm with reassurance: Connecting doesn't have to be physical. The small circle opened, and we quietly returned to the house newly linked with each other, our struggle with the harmonics transformed into a shared spiritual quest.

Back in the garden, we paired up and practiced singing scales, with one holding the drone note, the other moving up and down. Working with Wendy, I concentrated too much on singing the note, not expanding into harmonics, producing sounds that felt thin and strained. We fumbled around for a while, then gave up struggling to join Jilba who sat on the hillside overlooking the little pond dam. Soon Olwyn joined us and our voices began creating such wonderful harmonics that Viva was drawn closer simply to listen. Approaching, she found that the fluting harmonics she'd easily heard a few steps back had simply faded away. Walk back to where you heard them clearly, we told her, startled that the place of the listener was important. Playing around, we found that the optimum distance for hearing the harmonics was some thirty yards away. We'd had no idea how dynamic the connection was between audience and sound.

When it came time for us to practice individually, I was eager to see how well I could do without the other women's voices supporting me. But Sue, reluctant to go it alone, clung to my side, looking so lost that sending her away would be a major rejection. A bit self-consciously I droned away until I produced enough harmonic sounds that she became an appreciative audience. Why would she rather be a listener than a participant, I wondered, certain that the answer lurked somewhere in the lost orphan look her face so easily slipped into.

Trying to throw my voice a greater distance, I wandered across what would be a yard if Weerona were simply a farmhouse. Below me, Peter gripped the wire mesh fence of the tennis court, sounding with diligent concentration. Seeking shelter from the nearly noontime sun, I headed for the shade of an apple tree when Andrew approached. Placing his hands on my shoulders, he looked deep into my eyes and said, "Let's hear how you're doing, lass."

Lass was new, a term of endearment so gentle and unexpected that it threw me off balance; again I found myself melting in response to him. Lacking appropriate words, I responded to him with sound—which kept me from acting as silly and girlish as I felt.

At the close of the weekend, I'm asked why I'm in Australia and what it is that I'm writing—casual, friendly questions that suddenly rendered me incoherent. The quest that had brought me down under grew more mysterious each day. To say I was ready for a change of pace dishonored my deep longings, glossed over my sense of being called to take a journey of self-discovery. Trying to find my voice to talk about writing set off a new kind of fumbling as I struggled not to be glib or flip. Conscious of not wanting to trivialize my ideas or my work, I realized a profound difference between the near reverence I feel for words I mull over, polish, and use precisely and a sort of careless disregard for the words that just come tumbling out of my mouth. So often my spoken words are a defense; I've mastered sharp-tongued and witty. But questions remain: Why do I feel the need to deflect, to break the mood, to turn something serious into a joke? And, more important, can I get beyond my own defenses to whatever lies beneath?

Grateful for whatever clarity let me sing for Andrew, I could hug him farewell with true affection. What a relief to be spared any post-coital womb-tug of longing, the hopelessly female yearning to keep a living connection with whomever my body has chosen to take in, however strange, random, or inappropriate.

Wendy, who lived in Yackandandah, close to Beechworth, offered to give me a ride. She'd been a bit of a mystery, so time to get to know her better felt like a gift.

Once we began the long drive back, I jumped into exploring why sex shifted the dynamics of a relationship, as if talking to any woman in my circle. Was it just me, or was it true for women in general? I asked.

She knew immediately. "It's because we literally take them into our bodies," she said. "According to Indian teachings, when you have sex with a man, it places hooks of energy in your womb, energy so strong that the hooks stay for seven years."

For the rest of the long drive, I reveled in our easy openness as we laughed about the blunders we'd made, sharing tender moments and displaying our battle scars from the war of the sexes.

Perfect, I thought, as her car taillights disappeared into the autumn dusk. A campout had long been part of how my women's circle celebrated the Equinox. But none could compare with the time that the Autumnal Equinox came in March.

■ ■ ■

I returned with my ears attuned to hearing harmonics and, just like when I'd learn a new word and suddenly hear it everywhere, I found unexpected harmonics in the whine of the saws in the workshop, transforming their familiar sounds. A Steve Winwood CD that I knew by heart stopped me in complete amazement, as I listened, then listened again. Harmonics opened and took flight with the opulent order of a peacock's tail, sung like warbling magpies, and faded with the transitory precision of soap bubbles.

"Would you tell me if you can hear something?" I asked Quinn when he dropped by one afternoon. "Do you hear those fluty harmonics? What instrument makes those sounds?"

"I'm pretty sure it's a Moog," he said. "That kind of synthesizer is famous for creating those lovely harmonic bits of sound."

Sound—not only something we hear, but a synonym for strong, sturdy, healthy. Intact and unimpaired. Rational and practical. Ethical, moral, and truthful. A way of plumbing, measuring depth. A body of water.

My growing appreciation of sound could begin with a love poem to the Australian Broadcasting Company—which provided a grown-up version of the radio companionship that had been a childhood lifesaver. Opening aural doorways to the Middle East, Afghanistan, or the Balkans, ABC carried me to the beating heart of many a place I'd never visited. Modeled after the splendid BBC, it offered an invigorating, pleasing, and unpredictable mélange of music and news, interviews and stories, a wealth of programming that spoke to an Australian multi-cultural identity. As I sat at the computer or pottered around my Finch Street flat, ABC took me beyond my stone-walled lounge room and Beechworth's ruralness, linking me to the ideas and concerns of the whole continent and beyond. Sometimes an unexpected soprano aria would send me leaping for the "off" button, and, on occasions when I was feeling a bit surly, some of their audio adventures seemed to say, "Listen to this for your own good." But mostly I relished their daily adventures.

Then, one morning the radio filled my room with a rainbow of ethereal, swooping, and haunting sounds that danced between music and wind.

This piece floated delicate, soap-bubble harmonics, so subtle that I wondered if my ears really heard the hums and swoops and drones or if it were an audio mirage, the ethereal sounds of an aeolian harp as wide as the sky.

I stood next to the radio, anxious not to miss anything.

"That's 'Sky Song,' created by Australian composer Sarah Hopkins," said the clipped voice of the ABC announcer. "Part of the composition includes recordings she made of the wind blowing through telegraph wires in the outback."

Telegraph wires. Perfect, I thought. Telegraph poles and abandoned railroad tracks, forgotten cattle stations and rusting water tanks—detritus of decayed hopes and rusted dreams scattered across the Australian deserts.

"Sky Song" captured the plaintive voices of failed conquests: the sun and the sand had triumphed over metal pistons and diesel horses, leaving the eternal landscape of the didgeridoos humming beneath a jumble of windswept relics. Sarah Hopkins' pure harmonics turned sound inside out, revealing a clear, haunting, enduring beauty.

In it I heard the call of the Red Centre but had no idea how to answer it. Only later would I realize that wasn't to be a task for my mind, but another lesson in following my heart.

LURED BY LYRE BIRDS

Quinn arrived excited: He'd planned a surprise expedition to one of his favorite camping spots to give me a chance to see the "real" Victoria mountains, beyond Beechworth's foothills. I didn't require any urging. As Logan finished school and Tia gave her final piano lesson, Quinn and I blitzed through the grocery store, snagging camping provisions and piling the gear into the back of his truck with an easy working rhythm.

Worn to a Friday afternoon low, we drove in silent appreciation, soaking up the crisp autumn weather as the countryside opened into vast undulating fields. Gradually more and more dead trees, stumps, and snags pockmarked the rolling meadows—the ghosts of what once had been vast forests.

"Did all these trees die from some disease? Or was there a fire?" I asked.

"Settlers cleared most of them for grazing," Quinn said.

"You can still see a few of the natives clinging to the hilltops and valleys, the places too rugged to be plowed," Tia added.

"Not much of the land here is good for farming, but somehow people think they have to get rid of the trees," he said, resignation and sadness warring in his voice. Although he no longer worked as a landscape gardener, his palpable love of trees crowded the cab of the pickup.

"Clearing also altered the water table. Back when there was a vast forest, the eucalyptus, with relatively shallow roots, reached down just far enough. They kept everything in balance," he continued, "but now so many trees are dead."

A wistful sadness settled over us, perhaps sensing the ghosts of the trees. Or more likely the spirit of our grandfather, the gardener who taught us to love the scent of compost and leaf mold, who declared everyone should plant a tree for every year they lived as a simple tithe to the earth for the gift of life. He would have mourned the senseless tree murders.

In the back of the pickup, Logan sniffed the air with puppy-like anticipation, oblivious to the somber tone of our conversation.

"This isn't the only place with dead trees. The water table's rising all over Australia," said Tia, trying to melt the melancholy.

"So how does clearing off the trees raise the water table?" I asked, puzzled about how this could be. "Back in the states, clearing the land did just the opposite—creating the great dust bowl of the '30s."

"But that land was different," said Quinn. "This continent spent eons as a sea floor—and that means there's not much by way of topsoil. Without trees doing their transpirational magic, salts from the ancient sea floor dissolve. When they make their way to the surface, it's goodbye land. Take away the eucalyptus and the sea reclaims everything."

"See there? That bluish-green plant is saltbush. It pokes up when the salt starts rising to the surface," Tia said, pointing out clumps of the sadly familiar shrub along the roadside.

"But if salt is the problem, what about desalinization? Isn't that the tried-and-true way to make the deserts bloom?" I asked.

"They've tried. But the few experiments in de-salting the soils are too expensive—and mostly ineffective," she replied.

"So the trees really are the answer," Quinn said, tree-lover satisfaction smiling through his beard. "Now there are state-sponsored tree-planting programs; the native plants can restore the balance and keep this fragile layer of soil alive."

"Which means people have stopped clearing land and cutting down the trees?" I asked as more tree skeletons swept past the window.

"At least now it's against the law. The government recognized the problems that come from clearing the land and made it illegal," he said.

"But Australians can be a rough lot. Many of the old-fashioned pastoralists simply can't abide trees. It's almost an instinct with these blokes. They don't believe anyone should tell them what to do, so out they go and girdle or poison trees regardless," said Tia.

"It's hard to catch offenders like that. And, by the time a tree sickens, the damage is already done," Quinn said.

I felt a familiar pang of loss and a deeper appreciation for the Tree of Life, that living link between the upper and lower worlds, holding the power to balance earth and sunlight, water and air. My everyday tree meditation would hold a richer meaning from now on.

Outside the window, the pattern of cultivated fields lapping the smidgens of primal forest took on new meaning as the boot print of European colonialism. Deceptively pastoral, the cleared fields produce a fragile green, like the sickly pallor of Victorian ladies' faces. An apparently familiar sign—new green growth—concealed a different truth.

Somehow, the Koori people must have known theirs was not pastoral land. They chose not to plant crops. Instead, they traveled, following Earth's seasonal shifts, trusting in land's gentle bounty and their skill in reading the signs to find enough food to sustain themselves. I had only a foggy notion of how tribal elders used fire, unleashing it so that soon the velvet-footed wallabies and kangaroos came to graze on new forage sprouting on the fire-cleared land.

Yet I recognized one pattern with heavy-hearted familiarity: the way newcomers stamped out whatever they didn't understand, blind to the unfamiliar ways of nature's subtle graces. On the Great Plains, the outsiders replaced the buffalo with cattle, though only the buffalo knew not to calve when winter storms raged across the prairies.

I recalled a Colorado story when the old Arapahoe chief, Niwot, came upon a pioneer plowing a field in Boulder Valley. "Wrong side up! Wrong side up!" he exclaimed, watching with increasing horror as the blade turned up more and more soil. That early farmer had no clue that on the Great Plains, native grasses made the rich topsoil possible. Remove that webwork of roots, and the soil went away as well— washed away by pounding thunderstorms and blown by the prairie's howling winds.

European settlers drove Australia's native people to the edges, like the eucalyptus clinging to rocky crags and hillsides. And without the native knowledge-keepers, the soil of Earth itself slowly sickened.

Even so, all the settlers' subtle violence had not been able to destroy this valley's austere beauty; the hills stretched out like yearning arms, reaching to embrace us as we hummed along, dwarfing our little truck with somber majesty.

"Is there any hope?" I asked.

"Some studies say too many people already exist for the fragile Australian soil to support," Quinn continued, matter-of-factly. "There's almost no organic matter, no nitrogen, which is essential for just about every crop. In America, chemical fertilizers pump up the nitrogen to make up for the soil's lost vitality. That's impossible here, where we have just about zero petroleum reserves. Chemicals for fertilizers have to be imported, and they're just too darned expensive."

Quinn's casually relaying the history of this valley again conjured our long-dead grandfather telling stories of phosphates from fertilizers and laundry detergents entering the creeks and streams, patiently explaining how they nourished more algae than the fastest-running rivers could remove. Too much of a good thing is poison, he said, showing me where the nutrient-rich waters spilled into Lake Michigan, spreading eutrophication to all of the Great Lakes.

Did Quinn remember those stories? Did he know how our grandmother battled the Gary steel mills? Did he draw strength from the image of that brave woman facing down bulldozers, determined to defend the miniature orchids that grew in the Indiana dunes? In chronological time, he might not have heard our grandparents tell their stories. Our family moved away from them years before Quinn was born; he was only seven or eight when they died. Perhaps some inexplicable genetic magic gave him the power to hear the earth speak down under, I mused, until he interrupted my reverie.

"See that mountain jutting out? The one that looks like some giant sleeping beast? That's Mount Buffalo—named for its shape, not for the wildlife hereabouts."

"It's shaped just like a lump," I laughed.

"And what's the shape of a sleeping buffalo?"

"A lump!"

"Then Mount Buffalo is a fine name! After all, the settlers had to name it something," he chuckled. "They came looking for what they'd left at home, but instead of soft, fertile hills dotted with grazing cows and sheep, they found this stubborn landscape. Surprise! So it must be buffalo country." His slightly loony humor bubbled back to the surface as we left the beautiful, blighted valley and began threading our way up the large, granite, buffalo-shaped lump.

Glimmering white-barked ghost gum trees reflected the slanting autumn sun as we passed a turn-of-the-century mountain lodge that would have been at home in the Rockies. "I love coming here. It feels like such a relief," he said, nodding to include the mountain panorama. "Since all this is a wildlife sanctuary, it also preserves the native bush vegetation." We had entered a special bit of boundary land, a place preserved by its tenacious ruggedness.

As we unloaded the camping gear, I stumbled, calling the truck a pickup instead of a "ute." Logan enjoyed reminding me that ute is short for utility vehicle—but no one could come up with an explanation for the Aussie predilection for shortening words. Brekkie, tellie, and ute I'd grown accustomed to; the usefulness of others, like avo—afternoon—and chooks for chickens—still eluded me.

We pitched our three tents, creating a mini-village near a solemn park sign that proclaimed "Crow Crossing."

"Why did the crow cross the road?"

"To keep his pants up."

Quinn and I chortled our way through fractured why-do-crows-cross-the-road jokes, amusing ourselves with childhood references that left Tia and Logan baffled. Our explanation of American low-brow humor from Olsen and Johnson's *Hellzapoppin* to *Laugh-In* chicken jokes soon had them sharing in the laughter that signaled our getaway had well and truly begun.

Quinn and Logan took off to explore a nearby cave, Tia settled into a camp chair and a good book, and I wandered off to see what beckoned. An easy chair of granite boulders offered an orchestra seat for a bush bird symphony and I'd barely settled in when I heard an odd rustling sound near the ground. Hoping to spot a wombat, I silently shifted toward the scrabbling and found myself practically nose-to-beak with a huge, brownish black bird, trailing a sumptuous, peacock-like tail some three feet long. I instantly knew it was a lyre bird, even though its telling tail dragged the ground like the ball gown of some bush Cinderella. Stockier than a peacock, its swarthy feathers darkening almost to black, the lyre bird focused so determinedly on its pursuit of scrumptious nibbles that it was oblivious to my presence. For nearly an hour, I sat entranced as the elegant creature scratched like a barnyard rooster and gracelessly munched nameless bugs barely an arm's length away from me as I silently hoped for a glimpse of its smoky-feathered lyre fanned out in full glory. But, no such luck. Banquet finished, he scruffled farther into the bush, dragging his shrouded lyre tail behind him.

As I returned to camp almost breathless with excitement, Tia looked up from her book. "Did you see the lyre bird?" she asked casually.

"Then it really was a lyre bird? I've only seen pictures of them and had no idea they were so large."

"Actually this is only the second lyre bird I've ever seen— even though I'm an Aussie born and bred. They aren't that common any more—but Mount Buffalo is famous for them."

Quinn and Logan reappeared, surprising us. "We'd been set for a bit of spelunking, but the cave had other ideas," Logan said.

"We'd made our way to the mouth of the cave, but just moments after we entered it, both our flashlights just gave out," Quinn added. "I'd checked them beforehand, so their petering out at that moment seemed a pretty clear message. We skedaddled right back here."

"But we still need an adventure," he said before disappointment had a chance to register on Logan's face. "How about a hike up to a place called the Gallery? That's a scenic overlook near the top of the mountain."

Off we went to find the trailhead.

We'd barely started up the path when the heavy sound of huge wings made us freeze in our tracks. Thwoop. Thwoop. Thwoop. An equally startled lyre bird with a wingspan of some five or six feet flew just over our heads, down the hillside, and into the scrub below the trail. The startling flight sent my heart racing and Tia, the native, marveled. Watching one take flight was quite a rarity, since they usually stick to browsing on the ground. Clearly this particular lyre bird was showing off to impress the Yankee visitor, Tia decided, as we clambered up to a rocky ledge. The hills rolling out across the valley made a perfect echo chamber, and I strained to hear sounds of more lyre birds.

"Give it up," Tia said with a smile. "They're such shameless imitators that you'd never know if you were hearing a lyre bird or not. Sometimes they're called 'liar birds' because they're given to ventriloquist tricks and can mimic almost any sound. They've got a sly sense of humor."

Many an unsuspecting bush walker has been startled by a liar bird's dead-on imitation of a train whistle or the sound of revving motorcycles, she said. One legendary story told of a timber mill that used three blasts of a whistle to signal an accident and six blasts indicated a fatality. One day when six blasts sounded, workmen came running from all directions, only to discover that a lyre bird had convincingly mastered the whistle's sound. In another part of the bush, lyre birds convincingly sounded like goats, pigs, and chickens, amusing themselves with their own imitations long after the homesteader's barnyard had been abandoned.

Back at Crow Crossings, I thought I heard another lyre bird. Looking around, I spotted its now-familiar scruffling marks and decided to follow the tracks and listen. Spying the hulking bird, I chirped out a greeting sound, then another. Whatever whistle or squawk I produced, my feathered companion would casually toss a response over his shoulder, then continue digging with his sharp talons. Sometimes grumbling to himself, other times cocking his head thoughtfully before replying, he seemed a bit like my grandfather, the old gardener, preoccupied with weeding but still willing to banter a bit with any interested visitor. My lyre bird conversation ended when pelting rain forced me to seek shelter while my companion happily continued nibbling goodies he dug up in the bush.

Rain splattered our tents throughout the night and we awakened to a rainbow arching across the horizon in thin dawn light. The weather rapidly worsened. It looked too chancy for the hike Quinn had hoped for, and prudence dictated we'd best head for home. But, Quinn declared, we couldn't possibly leave without first climbing up for the view from the Horn—the highest point on Mount Buffalo. A stinging wind whipped warnings of an impending storm as we clambered up to the pinnacle. Low clouds shrouded the promised panorama as we stood pelted by icy soon-to-be-winter rain. Looking at a brass plaque that declared the Horn one of the highest points in the state of Victoria, we began laughing. Defying the storm, we'd clambered to the top—to reach just about the same elevation as my living room in Boulder.

■ ■ ■

Even halfway around the world, I'd not been able to leave behind one aspect of my former life—migraines. One began, as my migraines often do, with a throbbing in my right temple. The niggling pain was just a little headache: A couple of aspirins and it will go away, I told myself, trying to deny its presence. Then a burning spike stabbed through my right eye, a wrecking ball smashed against the top of my skull and a gigantic screw tightened the muscles at the back of my neck, sending my stomach lurching. I ran for the toilet as the first wave of nausea hit, filling my mouth with bile.

Wrapping ice in a towel, I lay down with the improvised cold pack on my forehead as the pain did its temple-pounding victory dance: "Ha! You thought you could get away!" the pain howled in triumph. The codeine, the last shot in my pharmaceutical arsenal, didn't even touch the pain before I threw it up, but it did make the queasiness more intense.

Outside my flat, winds swooped under the veranda, shaking the kangaroo-covered glass and rattling the windows like a crazed intruder determined to break in. As the sky grew darker, rain battered the little stone house with the intensity of a Calcutta monsoon, dropping the temperature to bone-chilling. I shivered, too sick to move from the bed, much less haul myself to the living room's gas grate, my only source of heat. Buckets of hail hammered the tin roof, as if I were trapped inside a gigantic, frozen snare drum. A cold cloth was no match for my throbbing migraine or the storm's assault.

It was the full catastrophe scenario: I was completely alone, paralyzed with pain, my house transformed into a dark refrigerator, slashed by lightning and battered by hail.

Feeling abandoned and sorry for myself compounded my pain as I struggled to decide what to do, vaguely aware that my brain wasn't at its best. It must be nine or so at night, so Quinn, the closest source of help, had long since shuttered the woodworks and gone back to the Woolshed Valley.

I hadn't seen a doctor in Oz, didn't even know the name of one. But there was the Ambulance Service next door. Was that an option? I contemplated the effort required to get out of bed and get dressed—or not. I didn't own a raincoat. Could I make it across the lawn with my new green polka dot umbrella? Would it protect me from the torrents of hail? Then, how would the Ambulance Service paramedics respond to a wild woman arriving in the teeth of a storm, hair tangled up like a terrified rooster, nearly incoherent from a migraine, speaking with a Yankee accent? Could I make any sense?

Imaging this scenario reawakened a childhood fear—being mistaken for a lunatic. For years I had nightmares about being locked up in a mental hospital, always trying to explain the reality of my situation—usually something about my father's cruelty, his drinking or threatening suicide—while the medical types listened impassively, secretly deciding the more emphatic I was, the more details I offered, the more confirmed they were that I must be raving. This old nightmare assumed new vividness in Beechworth, where the gentle lunatics of Mayday Hills, residents of the town's century-old mental hospital, wandered the streets providing odd bits of local color. The risk of being lumped in with the crazies when I was in too much pain to take care of myself re-created my oldest, sweaty-palmed nightmare.

Another terror: The migraine had settled in well beyond the point where oxygen could lift it, as it had on the flight down, and the odds of being shot full of something I was allergic to, in the Oz equivalent of an emergency room, loomed large. After three or four codeine, I doubted my ability to explain anything coherently. My pain-wracked brain could come up with only one solution: To avoid being hospitalized as a lunatic or sent spiraling off on some drug-triggered reaction, I had to know what particular medication or intervention to request. (Don't medicos everywhere think they know best? And who listens attentively to someone crazed with drugs and pain?)

Then, realizing that there'd probably be different drugs with unknown effects, I threw up again. After retching my insides out for the third time, I finally fell into an exhausted, restless sleep that diminished the pain enough that I could survive until morning.

With the dawn came the usual harsh, post-migraine interrogation: What had I done to "bring it on"? The cacophony of internal voices began attacking my judgment, questioning my thinking, undermining my trust in my self the moment the pain began to lift. Let's see: I had spent most of the previous day in a fine, frothing rage after reading two infuriating editorials in the supposedly "liberal" Melbourne paper. Before I arrived, Quinn had warned me I'd have a hard time dealing with the Aussie attitude toward women, and yesterday proved him right. Women seeking to end the casual display of pornographic pictures outside of virtually every news agency and milk bar—the little convenience stores found in even the smallest towns—were belittled for taking on a trivial topic when they objected to photos displayed to hype the *Hustler*-type magazines sold inside.

After ranting and raving about the similarities between sexism and racism to Quinn and his partner, I'd channeled my anger into a scathing letter to the editor, then returned to the workshop to read them my outburst. They both, bless their hearts, shared my outrage and applauded my approach. Apparently the connection between racism and sexism was an idea that has made little headway in the Oz consciousness. I mailed off the letter, proud of striking a tiny blow on behalf of women in Australia.

The postman brought sad news from the women's circle: a letter from Doris with an account of Jean's husband's gentle death that made me weep. Jean had shown the way to move into widowhood with awareness, making hard choices that defied society's—and her children's—expectations while staying attuned to her husband's needs as cancer slowly claimed him. Awed by her courage, I wanted to share her story.

The opportunity came that evening. Tia, her daughter, and I had called together a small gathering of women in Beechworth and, at our first meeting, I retold the story of how a ritual emerged spontaneously around his deathbed. We all wept sharing every woman's grief.

No doubt about it, as I reviewed the past pre-migraine days, I'd been feeling all kinds of emotions. So did that mean the migraine was some form of emotional whiplash? Could I avoid paralyzing headaches only if I anesthetized myself against outrage? Walled myself off from sorrow? Refused to open my heart? Was a migraine the price of feeling anything strongly?

Hopeless: I couldn't shut down my feelings, even if I knew with certainty that was the trade-off. So did that mean I was "choosing" the pain? Damn! How I hated all this wretched, New Age, blame-the-victim stuff—and I seemed to have absorbed it all, willy-nilly, into my very being!

The next day, as I wrestled with all my querulous internal voices, Quinn dropped by to see how I was doing. I fell apart, sobbing about how hopeless I felt, how stupid, because I couldn't figure out what caused these migraines.

He began telling me about the famous neurologist, Oliver Sacks, who said migraines are like an electrical storm in the brain. "Migraines still puzzle the whole medical profession," Quinn said. "No one knows the causes, although even the ancient Greeks wrote about them. All neurologists can do is chart the patterns of pain. And if no less an authority than the good Dr. Sacks can't come up with the answer, then why should you feel bad that you can't, either?"

Once again, I was grateful for Quinn, who almost always managed to come up with something both appropriate and loving. Once again, I realized that sharing my pain and uncertainty with him is a vital part of my healing.

"If you were a Koori, you'd have a ritual to deal with anger—even about stuff like sexism," said Joel. "All you need is the dark of the moon. That's the night of dark anger, the time when any woman could stand up and yell out all her tortured, personal grievances to the dark sky. She would rant and rail about any slight or misunderstanding. No one would argue. No one would answer back. Everybody would pretend they were sleeping or that they didn't recognize the woman's voice as they silently listened. There'd never be any retribution for what was said to the dark. She was just letting it be known how she felt—a good system that let people air their grievances and change their minds privately."

"Did that keep people from developing migraines?" I asked.

Joel didn't know. "Nobody ever mentioned headaches. Maybe that's a part of the modern world."

Neither story helped me decide what to do before my next migraine. It was comforting, however, to know that they weren't just from pollution, or stress, or some mysterious migraine-making combination from my life in Boulder. Because they recurred, I had to do something. But what? The codeine I'd depended on hadn't been able to touch the last hummer. I dithered.

A week later, along came a second migraine. It was a sunny afternoon, not in the midst of a nighttime monsoon, so I sought help from the local clinic, called, less-than-reassuringly, the Surgery, where the grandmotherly receptionist sat me down in an examining room corridor and promised to summon the doctor. He appeared in a flash, with a squashed-looking face, and a pinkish-purple scar running up one side of his nose that instantly made me wonder what was wrong with my vision. Looking at his barely repaired face hurt so much that tears filled my eyes. Was this migraine creating some new visual distortions? How could I ask if his face really was disfigured or warped by the blinding pain in my head? I decided to abandon the whole question.

Instead, I settled for telling him what I'd been prescribed, offering the nearly empty bottle, not reckoning that American and Australian drugs would have different names. My confidence was not increased as the doctor wrestled open the prescription bottle, examined the little white pills and then consulted a list of standard remedies. But at last I emerged with a prescription for Cafergot that worked like magic to knock out this particular migraine.

I had a new way to forestall migraines. Now I needed a way to recognize and overcome my initial denial that a migraine was tightening its painful grip. Why did I dither so long while the pain grew stronger? That puzzle seemed to apply to much more than my migraines.

Tracking

To survive in the bush, you must know your own footprints, an old Australian bush hand explained. That way, you'll know when you're going around in circles. In the heat and dryness, every anxious, unnecessary step brings you closer to dehydration—and death. The desert will defeat you if you're simply chasing your own tail.

Can I see my own psychic footprints, can I recognize when I'm chasing myself, repeating a pattern again and again? Simply slowing down long enough to notice footprints goes contrary to one of my family's patterns: Call it persistence, tenacity, or stubbornness, once you're on a course of action, there's no stopping. You have to keep on going, no matter what. Slowing down allows for doubting; doubting can make you quit, and all quitters are losers—full stop.

Not quitting is an Arctic survival strategy. In a world of cold and ice, moving keeps your heart pumping, your blood circulating, your lungs filling; if you stop to rest, you risk being frozen in place, blanketed alive by falling snow.

Trained to keep on trudging, even—or perhaps especially —when lost, overwhelmed, and confused, I'd stuck with a dodgy marriage for a decade, ignoring my husband's infidelities; having two daughters further slowed my urge to run. So much of his behavior, I now know, indicated a kind of unforgivable brutishness that would send most sane women fleeing.

My tracking skills are improving. I'm better at seeing the patterns of Falling for Mr. Unavailable and Looking for Love in All the Wrong Places. Listening to My Intuition, Appropriate Boundaries, and Asking for Help still need work. It's too easy for me to confuse them with the familiar bogeyman, Quitting.

Born trackers, Koori kids learn to read footprints earlier than ours learn their ABCs. By the time Koori children are toddlers, the footprints of tribe members are as familiar as their faces; telling the reptile footprint of a fat blue-tailed lizard from that of a tasty goanna is second nature.

Spotting the tracks of a couple who did not belong together provided great amusement; kids followed the footprints into the bush, then burst into the unsuspecting couple's tryst, dissolving into giggles. No adult could fault their tracking skills, and any would-be lovers had no grounds for complaint. My notion is that the Koori accepted impulsive couplings as a human foible, a big contrast to the shock of betrayal that infidelity triggers in our culture.

While the Koori's easy acceptance of sexuality seemed an appealing notion, I found it hard to reconcile the contradictions of a culture that painted cave walls with Mimis—figures that represented a good-humored wild, abandoned female sexuality—with one with deep roots in male polygamy. How could this be? It didn't take long to exhaust the resources of Beechworth's one-room library. Albury offered computer searches instead of a card catalog, but most all the accounts I found were written by white men. After reading a few things written by Europeans early in Australia's post-contact history, my distrust grew.

Some sites sacred only to women relate to a woman's cycle, said Val Stanton, a native woman, in a newspaper interview I read. "We call it the cycle of life," she said. "It relates from birth to death to all the things that are women's milestones in between. We have various stages of growing up," she said. Her explanation reminded me of our women's circle's rituals that celebrated marriage and pregnancy, the beginning of menopausal wisdom, or the anticipation of a grandchild.

"In my tribe, a daughter of a daughter—it might be the only daughter of an only daughter—has very great status," she continued. "We have elders, elder women, who have very high authority and we call them 'Almiuyuk-almiyuk' which means 'very important old women' and these women have as much status as elder men in certain places that might be, well, taboo, to other women or other older women, other elders." I wondered what it would feel like to have a special word for wise women, to be rooted in a culture that honored birthing daughters.

Val alluded to powerful women who controlled some sacred sites so closely that only they could even so much as mention their existence. Other women could not even utter the names of the sites and had to ask permission to discuss them among women.

Amid tales of magic stones, bones that brought death when they were pointed at someone, and mind-numbing anthropological charts of kinships systems, I found out that when a woman is widowed, the brother of her late husband takes her as his wife and provides her with food, shelter, and sexual gratification. But what did such women feel like? Was it a matter of pride or shame or something accepted as a matter of course? After a while, I realized that I wanted something which simply didn't exist. There were no Koori women's studies. Could I find a symbolic Rosetta stone that at once cracked open the mystery and brought all the disparate pieces together? I remembered how much was clarified for me by reading the story of the Balinese River Goddess.

The island of Bali is essentially a mountain; atop that mountain sits the temple of the Balinese River Goddess. The monks of the Temple of the River Goddess control an elaborate system of dykes and canals and watercourses, releasing some water on this side, some down this canal system, using the island's supply of fresh water selectively to flood the different terraced rice paddies that cover the mountainsides.

Somehow researchers from the National Science Foundation and a rice-growing institute decided that Bali would make a perfect case study. Surely all these great minds, coupled with computer models, would find the best way to distribute the water to maximize rice production, they reasoned. So they measured rainfall and soil moisture, the growing times of various rice fields. They used computers to model what conditions produced the best germination, the quickest growth, the highest yield of rice for each field, and finally reached their objective, scientific conclusion: The best way to distribute water was by the priests of the Balinese River Goddess.

Darned if I could find comparable fables for Australia.

Another way to learn was through the stories people told, through personal interviews that had yet to make it to the status of oral histories. Maybe that would be possible.

I went to Joel, my closest link to tribal people, and asked if he could put me in touch with some of the older tribal women.

"Probably not," he said. "One thing is pretty consistent from one tribe to the other. The men protect the women; they stand between women and the white culture. It's a role they've assumed since the first whites arrived."

"Do the men protect the women because they regard women as the weaker sex?" I asked.

"Be careful saying anything about the women being

weaker," he said with a rueful smile. "It's just the opposite. Women are so valued that men don't want the women to be bothered." I got the message: Some curious white woman from America, however well-intentioned, would definitely qualify as a bother. It would take more time than I had and some lucky personal contacts to learn much more.

As I wrestled with feeling deeply out of place, my nephew Logan arrived with unbridled enthusiasm and an armload of plastic buckets. "It's the perfect day to pick blackberries," he announced, "and I know just the place."

He led the way across pastures, ducking through barbed wire and hopping stones across a stream, narrating our journey with stories of dogs who had lived behind this fence and neighbors who, despite fences, understood the seasonal tug of blackberries.

"Are you sure these berries haven't been sprayed?" I asked.

"What makes you think any blackberries are sprayed?" he asked with laughing disbelief.

"Over by the gorge there's a sign saying not to eat the berries because they've been sprayed."

"Those signs have been up for years. But as far as I know, nobody's been doing any spraying."

"Why do they leave the signs up, then?"

"Probably nobody thought to take them down. Or maybe they thought they'd frighten the blackberries, you know, contain them by intimidation."

Grasshoppers hummed as we cautiously reached among the brambles for berries so ripe that they squashed into a rich purple stain with anything less than the most gentle touch.

"Darn, have to eat this one."

"These, too."

Logan made an admirable choice of patches to invade. Our conspiratorial smiles grew more purple as we gathered, munched, and licked the seeded sweetness from our fingers. Who cared that blackberries were an aggressive, weedy pest? We didn't even try to save enough for a pie.

"We'll come back for more tomorrow," he promised. The spiky blackberry canes nodded in agreement.

As we threaded our way back, I followed another track, awakened to a twelve-year-old-boy's eye view of the little town. Filled with the Huck Finn lure of Beechworth, I felt a huge longing for a childhood I'd never known.

What was it about this place? It made me yearn for answers to questions I could scarcely form.

My own dreams, usually reliable guides, seemed to have abandoned me. But I still hoped that perhaps the tales of this land itself, the Dreaming stories, would hold the answers. Another library mission yielded only stories that spoke about a specific part of the land, like this Wirangu story of creation:

> *When Tjuku first made Earth, there were the elements of earth, air, water and fire and inanimate plants and animals, but no people. Tjuku sent his spirit to Earth in the form of a falling star so big that it put a huge dent in the Earth (near what is now Eucla in the state of Western Australia) before it bounced into the sea. The falling star struck with such force that it awoke all the spirits of the creatures on Earth and brought them to life.*
>
> *As the fireball sank into the sea, it boiled the water around it. From the steam emerged two spirits: first woman (Minyma Tjukurpa) then man (Wati Tjukurpa). They met under the sea and swam around looking for a way to get onto land but were blocked by the cliffs (of the Great Australian Bight at the edge of the Nullarbor Plain). Eventually, each found one of the flooded tunnels that honeycomb the plain and open into the coast. They swam through the tunnels to underground caves where they could see the*

*light of the sun. Then they climbed to reach the surface and
emerged, born of Mother Earth. Wati and Minyam
Tjukurpa had many adventures traveling over the land creating things. But to learn more, you had to be an initiated
adult native to those lands.*

Occasional stories that linked the Dreaming and the
modern world popped up in surprising places, like *Australian
Geographic.* I was tickled by one account of a group of explorers
who set to explore Pannikin Cave, perhaps the largest underwater cave carved out of the limestone underneath the vast
arid and aptly named Nullarbor Plain west of Adelaide. Access
to the cave is a large hole in the desert floor that, from above,
looks like the drain hole it is. As the exploring team hauled
tons of underwater exploration gear, supplies, oxygen, and
communications equipment to the cave entrance, they forgot
about the spirits of the place. Expedition leader Andrew
Wight wrote:

*Strange things had happened back at the main camp.
First, a plume of dust shaped like a giant serpent appeared
in the otherwise clear blue sky over the camp. It hovered there
momentarily, then disappeared. The next day a willy-willy
(mini whirlwind) flattened one of our tents. Then a rainbow appeared, one end apparently rising dramatically from
the cave mouth.*

Few of the whites paid attention, but Maureen Young,
one of the last full-blooded Aborigines, visited the camp and
told them the events meant that a snake lives in the cave—
probably a real Rainbow Serpent. Rainbow Serpent, a promi-
nent figure in Aboriginal mythology, is both benevolent and
destructive and the bringer of storms. Maureen said that her
people always acknowledged the spirits and asked their permission when they wanted to camp somewhere for the night.
"The willy-willy indicates something might have been

displeased," she said. "Tell the cave: 'I want to go in and have a look; don't make me sick.'"

"Our cultural conditioning, however, prevented us from actually asking a spirit for permission to enter a cave," Wight wrote. "Later I realized that may have been a terrible mistake."

Expedition members paid no attention when a green and copper snake first appeared in the mouth of the cave, since it didn't do anything but watch them as they moved up and down the slopes to the underground access lake.

On the last day of their diving, the snake reappeared, lower down in the cave, and reared up as they passed. Then a freak cyclone struck, lashing the area with hurricane-force winds and dumping twice the annual average of rainfall in less than half an hour. Knee-deep water flooded into the underground cave, loosening rocks and boulders the size of camper vans, causing part of the cave to collapse. When the sides of the cave gave way, thirteen divers were trapped at the entrance of the underground lake as millions of gallons of water flowed into the cave over the next five hours.

Amazingly, no one was hurt. One small, brave woman went into the dangerously unstable cave and found a way through to those trapped below. Getting them out took more than thirty hours, since they had to climb out one person at a time, along a tortuous, single-file path to the surface, moving carefully to prevent further collapses amid thousands of tons of rock and rubble. Within a day, Pannikin Cave had experienced the kind of radical change that happens perhaps only once every ten thousand years.

Before departing, as expedition members gathered by the cave for a silent farewell, another survivor suddenly emerged—the green and copper snake. It slithered over to look at those who had been spared by the catastrophe, then returned into the darkness of the cave.

I couldn't tell which I identified with more—the snake, the rainbow, or the utterly transformed cave.

■ ■ ■

Quinn pulled me from my reading by announcing I had a phone call from Jilba in the joinery. "Got any plans tonight?" Jilba asked. "There's a fabulous women's group called Tiddas, playing a concert in the Vine Hotel—a funky little pub in the middle of the bush that likes to offer live music. It's simply amazing to get to see this group out here in the sticks. They're three young Koori women who are so good that they were the opening act for Sweet Honey when they played in Melbourne and Canberra."

"Of course, I'd love to come. And thanks for asking. Are they anything like Sweet Honey in the Rock?" I said, thrilled by the unexpected invitation.

"They do magnificent close vocal harmonies, accompanied by traditional clap sticks or shakers, and sometimes guitars. Beautiful, eclectic, compelling music—sort of like Indigo Girls with a social and political conscience."

"Sounds fantastic."

"I'll pick you up around six."

Jilba arrived with her van almost fully loaded. "Thought I'd round up the local women musicians," she said, nodding to Gemma and Molly, both accomplished singers and guitarists, and Dendi, a drummer who said she was learning to play the didgeridoo. "And then there's Ruby. Couldn't leave her out of the fun," said Jilba, indicating a dark brown bundle snuggled next to her hip.

"Where in the world did you get a baby wombat?" I asked, astonished as two shoe-button eyes peered up at me.

"She's an orphan. Her mom was killed on the road in front of my house. After that trauma, she was grateful to have someone pick her up and give her a cuddle. Go ahead, you can pick her up. She loves snuggles and likes to have her belly scratched."

I didn't need to be invited twice. Picking up the wiry-furred little creature, I was surprised by her heft—and the winsome way she snuggled her nose under my arm. "She's a pet, then?"

"She's definitely settled into the household. But it's a bit of a bother with a wombat in the house. They don't recognize walls."

"What do you mean?"

"Whenever a wombat encounters an obstacle, its instinct is to dig. So it digs through the walls if you don't catch 'em in time. It's murder on the woodwork. You should see what the back door looks like. But splintered baseboards are a small price to pay for having such a creature around."

"So then what do you plan to do with her at the concert?"

Jilba laughed. "Carry her with me, of course."

When we reached the Vine, her plan made sense. Far from a formal affair, this was a country pub concert, where a few tables had been pushed to one corner of the dining room, clearing space for a few dozen chairs that faced an impromptu stage.

As the three dark-skinned, dark-haired young women stood up to the mikes, the room roared, hooting, clapping, and stomping a rowdy welcome that loosened the last hold-outs from the bar. As clear and inevitable as the magpie's liquid trill, their harmonies used simple words:

As I walk on this land of my people's dreaming,
I can feel the spirit of the winter tree.

Theirs were love songs to the earth and its seasons, to the clouds, lakes, and trees and their people whose lives entwined with the strong eucalypts and clear blue waters.

Koori woman, where are you going?
Koori woman, where are you going?
Koori woman, where are you going?
Going home to my mother land,
Where my heart can be at peace,
Be at peace. . . .

Koori man, where are you going?
Koori man, where are you going?
Going back to my sacred land—
No more fighting the white man's war,
The white man's war.

As Ruby the wombat snoozed in Jilba's ample lap, I felt the strength of the earth's grounding for me, too. Like silt carried by a river, their harmonies slid their stories into my being.

"What is that power of words and music intertwined?" I asked as we headed back to Beechworth.

"It's just magic, pure and simple," said Gemma.

"Whatever it is, I'd like a bit more," Dendi added. "Let's go to my place. I'll put on the kettle and we could make a bit of music together. You did bring your didj, Jilba?"

In a few minutes, a fire warmed the kitchen, hot tea had been dispensed and Gemma pulled out her guitar as Dendi and Jilba added fresh wax to the mouthpieces of their didgeridoos. "The women of Tiddas—they're all Koori, right?" I asked, "but no one played the didgeridoo. Is this a Koori cliché or something?"

"Mostly, they're singers, I guess. And there may be some tribal restrictions about it. Lots of people have big taboos around the didgeridoo. Some say only men can play them and others don't care at all," said Jilba.

"Then what about women like you, who have no tribal ties but go ahead and play it anyway?"

"Women who play the didgeridoo who aren't supposed to can be cursed," said Jilba. "And do you know what the curse is?"

Three pairs of eyes awaited my reaction.

"The curse is—they'll have only sons, no daughters."

We all collapsed in laughter.

"How about a drum for you?" Dendi asked, rolling in a big conga from her lounge room.

"In truth, I'd rather hold the baby wombat, if I may."

"Perfect! Now you can have the ultimate Australian experience—a woman's didj concert while you cuddle a baby wombat," said Jilba, handing over a drowsy, content lump of wiry fur. Stroking Ruby's firm, warm belly, I felt a gentle acceptance from this far-from-wild creature, so self-contained yet people tolerant. The didgeridoo calls echoed off the kitchen walls, transforming it into a wild women's cave, our songs a celebration.

That evening's unexpected initiation prepared me for the next step in my journey.

INTO THE RED CENTRE

My intrepid friend Robin, sharing stories of exploring the deserts on camelback, helped me understand why the Red Centre is considered quintessentially Australian. Not only does its sheer acreage dominate the map, but its stories of struggle against the elements, of triumph over privation, are the keys to some aspects of the country's identity. Lacking the promise of a camel expedition, however, I'd quietly abandoned the idea of seeking out a desert trek until one sunny day when Robin arrived at my doorway gleaming with excitement.

"Remember my telling you about my friend Jean?" she asked, hardly pausing for me to nod before bubbling on. "Jean grew up living with the natives in the outback where her father worked for the Royal Flying Doctor Service. And now her book's just being published."

"An autobiography?"

"No. It's the story of her father's life, about how much they learned from living with the natives in the desert for years and years."

"And . . . ?"

"And—if she can scout up twenty interested people, she'll organize a huge desert trip. She'll include on-the-road tutorials from a botanist, a geologist, and an astronomer to really learn about the desert as we follow the routes flown by the Doctor Service—but driving instead of flying. The whole trip is planned as a special sort of book launching, one that celebrates her love of the desert."

A real desert encounter—especially one that replaced a white wine and runny cheese author's reception—seemed perfect. "Where would we go?"

"Along the Birdsville Track. Yulara. Cloncury. Balcanoona. Urandangi and Oodnadatta," she continued, rattling off the unfamiliar names like incantations as her arms arced a four-thousand-mile circle of Australia's heartland desert.

Each place name vibrated with meaning for Robin, while I felt like the time when I'd successfully asked for directions in Venice—and then been bombarded with directions and comments in Italian.

"I've only heard of Alice Springs and Ayers Rock and don't even know what's there," I said, clueless about desert details.

"I don't know much about the area, either. I've mostly been along the Birdsville Track—that's where I did my first camel expedition. But I can guarantee you the trip will be great. Jean is quite the old bush hand—she must be seventy-something now—and has organized lots of desert trips. I've done a couple and I always learn heaps just spending time with her."

"We'll go to the Back of Bourke!" she exclaimed, reducing us both to hopeless laughter. Back of Bourke and Beyond the Black Stump are Aussie slang for anyplace beyond the boondocks, way into the toolies, all the way to whoop-whoop, the raggedy edge of the world.

For Robin, adventure and learning were virtually synonymous. After living in England, Denmark, and Peru, when she and her husband moved to Australia, it was as if Robin had enrolled in a self-directed study course in cultural melding. Her new homeland was a country of immigrants, she said:

"Even the skinny little Beechworth phone book offered introductory instructions in more than forty languages, including Hindi and Farsi." Soon she began working at an immigration center, helping newcomers settle, absorbing their stories, and being touched by their dreams. Not content simply to savor this zesty cultural stew, she wanted to share her enthusiasm and soon began writing for newspapers, then hosting and scripting her own radio show.

While Robin vibrated with the energy of the ever-eager scholar, I got practical and found a shop where I could send an international fax and fired off a query to a stateside magazine. Writing assignment in hand, I could abandon worrying about costs and conjure visions of stimulating campfire conversations and sleeping under the starry desert sky.

We booked our reservations.

Come departure day, Quinn drove us to the Albury railroad station where we'd join the rest of the group.

"Because Victoria and New South Wales couldn't come to terms on railroad gauges, Albury has the distinction of having the longest platform in all of Australia," he explained. "Passengers from one state traversed the platform to a whole 'nother railroad."

"A great bit of trivia—and you get bonus points for being utterly irrelevant," Robin laughed. "But we're camping out and occasionally staying in motels, not taking the train. The railroad station is just an easy-to-locate gathering place."

Unloading our gear, we simultaneously spotted a gigantic, shiny black Greyhound-sized bus. My heart sank as the three of us exchanged glances. Whatever mode of transport Robin and I had been expecting, this behemoth was definitely not it.

"Looks like the trailer it's towing behind has a full field kitchen," Quinn said.

"We'll have lots of elbow room," Robin added gamely.

"No trip would be complete without one of those," said Quinn, nodding toward an older man videotaping the looming vehicle. "It's not too late to change your mind," he offered, eyes twinkling in amusement. Knowing we'd come too far to back out, he was enjoying our mutual dismay.

As Robin and I clambered aboard, only Jean offered a welcoming smile; our fellow travelers, a wall of tight-jawed, aging Anglo faces, squinted disapproval as we edged toward the few remaining seats. Jean introduced the driver, the cook, the teaching staff, and Rosemary, a physician who'd just returned from three years of living in Fiji. With travelers averaging seventy or older, an experienced field doctor seemed a wise addition, I thought, little suspecting I'd be the first to need Rosemary's assistance.

The back-of-the-bus seats we'd earned with our procrastination were ours for the first leg of the trip. They came with extra jouncing and an exhaust fume bonus so that by the time we neared Port Augusta, I had a screaming migraine. Green, queasy, and disoriented, I slowly realized that we'd stopped at our first Flying Doctor Base, one that adjoined a hospital.

"Do you suppose I could get some oxygen?" I asked Rosemary, explaining I'd been battling a migraine and nausea triggered by my own peculiar allergic reaction to the exhaust fumes.

Grabbing my hand, she led me inside the hospital calling, "Basin! Basin!

"That always brings 'em running. No one likes wiping vomit up off the floor," she said good-naturedly.

Resting my throbbing head against the cool tile walls, I watched a nurse dash in as predicted, enameled bowl in hand. Within minutes I was lying down, ice pack on my head, given an injection of Cafergot, and left in soothing semi-darkness as the Flying Doctor Base tour ended without me.

While the tour staff had planned a system of regular seat rotation that required each pair of seatmates to move back a row each morning, my penchant for vomiting instantly earned us seats in the front of the bus. I was grateful.

Tall, long-necked birds gallumped alongside.

"If it's an exhalation of larks and a murder of crows, what's the collective noun for emus?" I asked.

"Must be a flounce of emus," Robin said, smiling as the ungainly birds raced alongside us, gaping mouths sounding inaudible alarms.

Although they can muster a lethal kick, I couldn't manage to feel menaced by long-necked critters with bustles bouncing in a parody of panic.

The gigantic coach halted alongside a garbage dump and we all filed out. We'd reached the first of many informative stops along the way. "Oysters and other marine creatures ruled over this corner of the desert some fifteen to twenty million years ago in one of the episodes when Australia's center became an inland sea," said Maurie, the on-board geologist. "Not far away in West Australia, researchers have identified the world's oldest exposed rocks, some dating back four billion years, and here you see probably the youngest rocks to be found anywhere in the country. They've survived here because of ultra-dry conditions," he said, thrilled with the geological wealth.

Robin and I were amused that these fossils survived beside what's now the town rubbish tip. Judging by the odd glances from residents who came to dump their trash, the ancient oyster beds weren't a major tourist stop.

"What kind of an omen is this for our trip?" I asked Robin.

"Clearly, we've got nowhere to go but up," she laughed as we clambered back into the coach. Soon silver-blue saltbushes began melding into a more typical desert landscape as we headed north.

■ ■ ■

Two days before we arrived in Curdimurka, South Australia, there had been a black-tie ball. More than two thousand people had flown from Adelaide to a rough-and-ready airstrip. There they pitched camp in the desert, put on their fancy clothes, and celebrated a benefit bash for the efforts of Australia's National Trust to preserve Curdimurka's rustic old wood and stone railroad station.

The posh revelers were gone. Only bush latrines—"dunnies"—and stacks of black plastic trash bags remained of what, for a weekend, had been the largest city within a thousand miles. As rain clouds swirled across the flat, barren landscape, Curdimurka returned once more to a deserted railroad station alongside an ad hoc airstrip.

An overnight rain released the smell of limestone and turned the ground into a sea of gluey mud. The mud stuck to my shoes so determinedly that the further I walked, the taller I grew. Returning from the dunnie, I was a clumsy, lead-footed giant, my right eye swollen shut from bug bites.

"Welcome to bush camping," said Robin, her laughter seeming to halt the rain. The railroad that once ran through Curdimurka is still called the Ghan, a rough homage to the historic role of Afghan traders in opening up the desert to trade and travel.

Whoops of excitement drew us over to the Ghan's old "sleepers"—railroad ties—where a lazy lizard more than a foot long sat soaking up stored warmth, unperturbed by the curious travelers humming with excitement. Judy, the botanist, was summoned over to identify it. "It's called a pinecone lizard, named for the texture of its fat tail. They're part of the family of blue-tongues," she said. The Australians all nodded and shuffled away. I remained curious about its blue tongue.

At Curdimurka the landscape offered a study in dryness, with a few striking tropical accents, like the palm trees that grew scattered along the roadside. The softly chattering palms were a botanic legacy of date-eating camel drivers who discarded pits along the track more than two hundred years ago, Judy explained. Confronted with so much desert, early European settlers recruited both camels and drivers from the Middle East. Ranging over most of the arid interior, Afghani traders brought provisions, news, and necessities to people in the outback, marking their paths along the landscape with date palms and fuchsia clouds of rosy dock, seeded from the stuffing of their imported saddles.

Two legends explain the name Curdimurka. One is about people who came through a hole in the sky and couldn't get back, the other about wild-eyed creatures who prey on unwary travelers. I was glad Jean waited until daylight to tell us. As we moved from one part of the desert to another, I sensed something hidden and mysterious, a subtle contrast to the frankness of the deserts of the American West. Examining whatever maps I could find, one thing struck me: the difference between the surface and what lay barely hidden, just beneath—the phantom lakes, ghost rivers, and innocuous-looking holes that open into shape-shifting caverns.

Maps show Lake Torrens, Lake Frome, the Playa Lakes, and Lake Eyre North and South. Tribal people speak of Lake Dieri that once covered more than a hundred thousand square kilometers. All are enchanted phantoms, dormant and invisible, that come to life only with rainfall then vanish into the sky. The Dimantina, the Thompson, the Bourke are invisible rivers threading through the Centre. Even the maps showed a dreamtime geography that could reshape overnight, a dry landscape that echoed water's power to appear suddenly, transform, reshape, and dissolve.

Walking the shores of Lake Eyre, the salt and sand underfoot crunched musically as Robin and I chose a vantage point to watch the shifting mirages over the purple-blue lake. Beneath my feet, I seemed to feel the traces of ancient watercourses and rivers, vast features so blurred with time that they are evident only in satellite pictures taken from space. Here phantoms were real, mirages a part of the landscape in this desert of sparkling white sand.

The whole continent is a sort of basin, gently tipping toward the South Pole, rimmed with mountains to the north and the east. At the bottom of the basin drain lies Lake Eyre, about fifty feet below sea level, the most enduring of the capricious salt lakes that form in the low spots of half a million miles of desert, then vanish in the sun. Water is a powerful shaping force in the desert; only Koori feet can hear its promise in the wind or trace its song lines across the sandy vastness.

Years later, back in Boulder, I could understand when one Koori man told me of being taken from his desert family as a child. Brought to a mission school on an island off the north coast, his body shrouded in clothing for the first time, he missed the physical comfort of sleeping with his relatives like a big puppy pile, longed for the messages received by his skin. "Your skin is your body's largest sensory organ," he said, "and living in the desert, you take in information from your skin, messages about your environment that's hard to put words to."

The well-meaning missionaries thought they were giving him a gift with clothes that scratched and bound him, believed they were doing something good by making him sleep in a flat bed with harsh sheets. "As soon as the lights were out, I got out of bed and shed those pajamas. I'd go lie down on the floor, with my hands in a little crack where the wall didn't quite meet the floor, and fall asleep where my fingers could still feel the air moving."

■ ■ ■

In truth, I'd never heard of Australia's Great Artesian Basin and, standing on the edge of it, was startled to learn it's the earth's largest, an area the size of France, Spain, and Portugal. The Brobdingnagian depression that is much of the Red Centre includes an aquifer that's capped by a rocky layer of shale and silicrete as impermeable as a kitchen sink. Floods and rain send water along the basin's higher, more absorbent edges, where it seeps along a fragile underground web of cracks and fissures and, much like the system that creates the geysers of Yellowstone, forces the water up through the fractures to the surface. Over time, the dissolved salts, silica, carbonates, and other minerals have created clusters of mounds at the mouth of each artesian spring; some reach a hundred feet or more above the lake floor; others have spread out flatter, creating raised drinking fountains. Each mound spring has a unique shape, each is the heart of a living system of rare plants and uniquely adapted fauna. I'd seen similar pools at the Yellowstone hot springs, but here the pools and fountains were more than a geological curiosity; they held fresh, drinkable water.

Throughout the desert, any fresh water source is something to be treated with respect, even reverence; dependable drinking water can spell the difference between life and death. In Koori folktales, fouling a waterhole is an act that brings swift retribution from the spirits of the spring. Nowadays, cattle ranchers sinking bores to water their livestock endanger the fragile flow to the mound springs in the process, Maurie, the geologist, said.

As I left the eerie artesian landscape, dune after rolling red dune wore a gauze-like cloak of pea-green vegetation, broken by stands of blood-red desert peas, their centers gleaming like black insect eyes. The air filled with the croak of frogs—a special arid zone species that burrows underground to escape drying out and emerges only when it can feast on insects displaced by showers. A touch of rain in the past two weeks had produced this rare biological extravaganza, which I regarded as a welcoming gift.

Among the rolling hills covered with soft scrub, we stood at the edge of an ochre pan. "Here's a spot where, for eons, Aborigine have come to paint their bodies for ceremony," said Maurie. Touching the pale, moist ochre, I conjured up dark limbs painted with stories told in harlequin dots and zigzags of red and yellow ochre, versions of the dot paintings I'd seen in Colorado, with skin as their canvas. Did they absorb another form of earth wisdom through ochre on their skin? I wondered. And what do we absorb from the factory chemicals we use on our skin?

Robin had similar thoughts. "It would make my life a lot more interesting if some of our fellow passengers used ochre instead of their standard face paint," she whispered as we encountered Shirley, who faithfully applied her Eternally Surprised Eyebrows each morning. "Why wear makeup for hour after hour of driving through the desert? And I'd be wildly grateful if they'd skip the perfume."

Maybe I should explain that when Robin and I were first introduced to our fellow passengers, Robin's British accent instantly pigeonholed her as the little Pom, or Limey, while I was the lone Yank. Since we were easily categorized by the other passengers, we were easily dismissed, and being ignored suited our quiet, often introverted selves just fine. Huddled up together in our shared seat, we passed notes and whispered observations of our fellow travelers like a couple of junior high school exiles.

When the coach stopped for meals or sightseeing, the two of us would go separate ways. Robin headed off, bright and curious as a newly hatched chick, to return to share her tasty observations. Although encumbered with notebook and camera, I still secretly hoped that, this time, in this place, the land would come up to meet me, like in the old Irish blessing. The desert trek settled into a pattern: hours and hours of driving, broken up by stops at public toilet blocks and mealtime pauses. Energized by the promise of some new informational tidbit, we usually managed to perk up a bit when one of the lecturers offered an impromptu on-board tutorial. Awaiting the next chance to disembark, Robin and I watched the passing desert, dozed, or amused ourselves by critiquing the food, our fellow passengers, or the provincial, authoritarian coach driver.

Our fellow coach captives not only provided amusement but a host of small-scale irritants: Ludwig's Prussian exhortations to learn about astronomy. Irena's plomping in a seat and refusing to move, all cloying sweetness and would-be beguiling smiles, an exaggerated two-year-old act that seemed particularly unbecoming in a woman over seventy. Marie, who flattened every experience, whether soup or scenery, down to a single word: "beoooudyfooool."

Pitching camp each evening brought out the other bored and restless travelers, eager to interfere in the guise of helpfulness. As two women traveling together, Robin and I were favored targets for the men who needed to tell us how to pound in our tent stakes or the women who wanted us to change the way we buttered our bread.

Francie, the queen of unsolicited advice, felt obliged to provide me with instructions on how to stand up a broom after sweeping out our tent, when it was time to eat lunch, and whether or not I'd chosen the right slice of bacon.

One morning, Francie mounted her most direct attack as I padded around the camp barefoot, grateful for grass underfoot: "Look at those bunions," she exclaimed, pointing to my feet. "You wouldn't have had bunions like that if you'd put cotton wool between your toes when you were a child, especially if you have a long first toe like you do. You need to put cotton wool between them every day to keep them straight. I always did and that's why I don't have bunions today."

"Guess I'm stuck with these feet, since it's too late to go back and redo my childhood," I mumbled, feeling stupid for letting Francie's attack touch me enough to make me feel bad. I turned to see Robin, who'd witnessed the whole scene.

"Francie's out of control. She's now making stuff up to get to you," she chortled, barely containing her laughter as she led me away. "You don't even have bunions."

"She blindsided me," I sputtered, still furious. "I wish I'd been able to come up with some snappy comeback."

"Even responding to her is hopeless. No mere words, no facts can puncture that woman's rind of self-satisfaction."

"I just don't get it. What motivates someone like that?"

"Sometimes new things bring out the worst in people. I'm willing to bet that this trip is the first experience of camping out for these folks. Not to mention taking in all we've seen, after carefully limiting your life to a rural Australian farm."

■ ■ ■

The journey offered another, simpler, way to be bugged. The desert, I quickly learned, is a haven for insect aficionados. The primary inhabitants of the interior, in both variety and sheer numbers, are the bugs. Seemingly immune to drought, they must always be prepared for the lethal havoc of the desert's irregular floods. Anthills are surrounded by protective dikes. Termites build distinctive red towers that stand like stalagmites characterizing the deserts of the Northern Territory.

My appreciation for the insects dimmed as the number of blowflies increased. The almost automatic flick of the hand to sweep flies from eyes, ears, and nose is lightheartedly called "the Aussie salute." As the landscape grew drier, the flies became more determined—since the moisture in our eyes or noses might offer the nearest fly oasis for hundreds of miles, Judy the botanist explained. My role in the insectivores' grand scheme of things didn't thrill me.

The scrubbed-looking hills, cut with ravines, revealed soils in hues varying from a screaming orange to a dried-blood maroon as we approached Oodnadatta, a name that's a corruption of the native word for the mulga scrub that had once covered the landscape. "Now there's nothing, not even the mulga, largely because of overgrazing by the likes of the Sydney Kidman stations," said our guide, Jean, not bothering to conceal her contempt for someone who is careless with the desert's resources. "Kidman—Nicole's daddy—controls an area roughly the size of Texas where cattle graze—or scrounge. This ranch's vegetation is so sparse that the cattle stations allot more than two hundred fifty acres per head—ten times higher than on the leanest American rangeland.

"The devastation we're seeing is due to European settlers, whose cultural taught them that nature was here to serve man. Their job was to subdue the earth. And they came with agricultural practices suited to harnessing the land's fertility," Jean continued.

"Quite the contrast to the Koori, who draw their spiritual strength from the land. From birth, they each have their own personal earth connection. And as a group, they believe it's their sacred duty to leave the earth as it was on the first day of creation. Too bad that lovely idea has worked toward their detriment."

"How so?" I asked, puzzled that spiritual strength would work against you.

"Ever hear of *terra nullis?* It's Latin for vacant land, how the Brits decided if a land was inhabited. Nothing as simple as people. What counted was buildings. No buildings meant a place was up for grabs," said Jean. "And since, technically, Australia was not inhabited, that meant that the dark-skinned beings they saw weren't really human. Couldn't be, according to *terra nullis.* And that set the stage for a lot of nasty mischief."

"The Maori in New Zealand fared so much better," Robin added. "The Maori traditionally carved those beautiful long houses—so their island was deemed inhabited. Eventually they got treaty rights."

We stopped for lunch outside the Oodnadatta country store where eager kite hawks swooped down, dive-bombing our picnic tables for any scrap of food. Robin and I took turns throwing bread crusts, watching the majestic hawks circle and dive like a flock of gulls.

"Did you notice those yellow balls along the roadside?" asked Judy, the botanist, joining our table. "They look like relics from some abandoned ping-pong tournament but they're melons, or camel melons, called that because they're so bitter that only camels will eat them," she said.

"We're surrounded by biological relics of a climate shift some forty-four million years ago," she continued, drawing a fascinated audience as she warmed to her topic. "Desert oaks look like a cross between a bottle brush and a cactus but they're the advance troops of a biological invasion," she said, waving at the tall improbable trees. "They minimize water loss by foregoing true leaves. What looks like needles are really stems. When Australia separated from Antarctica, a circumpolar current developed, polar ice sheets grew, and temperatures dropped. Rain forests retreated north as the desert oaks, eucalyptus, and grasses began moving in, where they remain to this day."

Her impromptu lecture left me wondering about the preternatural energy of living relics, of plants that had learned to thrive in the most inhospitable conditions. Not to mention the incongruous camels.

Far more familiar were the kangaroos. Natural energy conservers, they stretch out in any available shade, motionless in the mid-day heat, mimicking the shape of dead scrub on the horizon. I couldn't help noticing that here almost all the roos are a dusty red, not the stone gray of their cousins in the Victoria hills.

"Desert plants sprout within a few days of rain; kangaroos conceive within the next two weeks," Judy said. "The females have two wombs, so they can jump on any opportunity to reproduce. Which means the better the grazing, the more kangaroos."

The dynamic link between the roos and the rain was another reminder of why I love learning the intricate ins and outs of nature.

■ ■ ■

Near Uluru, the red desert, a badlands of scrub flats, the vegetation grows so low that eagles build nests on telegraph poles. The tallest things on the horizon are clumps of spinifex grass that grow from six to more than twenty feet across. Often hollow in the center, the spinifex—a plant with leaves akin to bayonets—provides perfectly defended nests for snakes, emus, and lizards.

"Welcome to Aboriginal Land" says a sign; "Uluru National Park and the Ayres Rock Resort is open from 6 a.m. to 7:30 p.m." It closes to give the Rock a chance to rest, said some wag in the back of the coach. Built in 1984 and modeled after U.S. national parks, Uluru has all the amenities: three hotels, facilities for disabled visitors, campgrounds, art galleries, a swimming pool, and a museum, as well as its own fire department, police station, and Flying Doctor Base. Although we were camping out in our musty little canvas tents, this could hardly be called a wilderness experience.

Come dusk, nearly everyone headed for the viewing area, Sunset Strip. More than twenty buses disgorged German, Japanese, Danish, Italian, and English tourists, as well as throngs of Australians on holiday, all eager for the evening's Rock Show.

The enormous Rock, an almost living presence emerging from the flat desert floor, seemed to emit a low-level hum. An evening squall created a rare and breathtaking sight—Uluru highlighted by a rainbow, revealing a subtle spectrum of colors on its sculpted surface. Lightning cracked as a helicopter and a plane droned by. Miles away, Kata Tjuta appeared as a distant, spectral Stonehenge shrouded in mist and rain.

Robin and I used our binoculars to spot the chain that helps climbers reach the top of Uluru, trying to decide what we would do the next day.

To climb or not to climb had been the question for days—and no one lacked for advice. Signs cautioned visitors to begin a climb early, warned them not to try the climb with a heart condition, asthma, vertigo, dizziness, or fear of heights—all in five languages. Some people had been training for weeks for the steep climb up the face of Uluru. There are other options, too: dawn plane rides, helicopter flights or, my favorite, the

Harley tour. Its motto: "Ride a legend to see a legend." Robin and I postponed our decision until morning.

A nearly invisible route curved around the dunes, insinuating itself, snake-like, into the sandscape. This road supplanted the old straight-line scar across the plains. Naturalizing the park included replacing the road to Uluru and the old resort made famous by the search for Desara Chamberlin, an incident brought to America's attention by Meryl Streep's film *A Cry in the Dark*. When the old resort hotel and airport were relocated, the area was revegetated flawlessly.

But that chain remained, threaded through posts hammered into the rock. With no chain to hold onto, no casual tourist could make it more than a thousand feet straight up above the desert floor. By 9 a.m., thousands of people swarmed around the base of rock, most determined to haul themselves up, hand over hand, along the chain.

A sign declared that the Anangu people, those to whom this land is sacred, do not climb the Rock. That made our decision easy. Robin and I opted to walk along the base of this massive oval of sandstone, choosing the path of those who have lived with Uluru for more than twenty thousand years.

Uluru records the activities of Mala, the first rock-clambering hare wallaby, at the time of creation. The tourist chain lift cuts across Mala's fabled path. One bell-shaped opening, a sacred site for women, is known as the pocket of the hare wallaby. Such especially sacred sites are off-limits to visitors. The sight of Uluru speckled with clambering visitors like ants assaulting a sugar cube did not reassure those like me who were concerned about the sanctity of particular spots.

The base of the Rock, fluted and scalloped by wind and water, holds countless caves, some smaller than a fist, others large enough for a tribal gathering. Some caves reveal white walls or golden interiors, the result of subtly varying composition of the rock itself. Others seem like a chorus: mouths with delicate uvulas hanging from the ceiling, far more rounded and dainty-seeming than anything I'd call a stalactite.

Every curve and fissure seemed to sing with mythic meaning, holding, celebrating the continuous creativity the Koori call the Dreaming. Every geographic feature holds a story, but only those who are keepers of a story may share it. We were grateful when we encountered a park guide who told us that Mutitjulu (Maggie Springs) is a permanent waterhole that's the home of a sacred water python. We sensed the magic of its spot, even though the guide could tell us no more of the story.

An ancient hunter's lookout, an almost-cave-like overhang, shelters hunters awaiting any game heading for a drink. The cave's interior walls are decorated with designs as old as the tribal artisans who painted them, embellishing animal forms they saw within the rocks. Painting sacred designs as they watched and waited, these artisans evoked the animals and their life-sustaining roles. It's impossible to date Australian rock paintings because they're constantly renewed whenever a sacred site is used; repainting the ancient designs is an integral part of the rituals.

Uluru's spectacular red color, from iron oxide, is a sort of rusty, oxidized rind over an interior of sandstone conglomerate that varies in hue from gray to gold. Why this huge piece of sandstone survived more than five hundred million years of erosion while its surroundings were pummeled to orange dust is a mystery that adds to the monolith's impact. Maurie was not the only geologist stumped when asked to tell the story of this spectacular dune.

I wished I knew how to ask the hare wallaby or the water python.

• • •

The clustered dome formations that towered in the distance beyond Uluru were called Kata Tjuta—"many heads"—a name that conveys the formation's sense of giant Earth spirits coming together for a confab. But the evocative native name was ignored; when explorer Ernest Giles reached Kata Tjuta, he dubbed the highest "Mount Olga," to honor Queen Olga of Wurttemberg. Since then, all thirty-six of these beehive-shaped formations are casually called "The Olgas."

This was only one of countless times that white explorers down under displayed their distressing fondness for naming their "finds" after political patrons. William Gosse, the first white man to reach Uluru in 1873, named it after Sir Henry Ayers, the premier of South Australia—a man who, as far as I could tell, never set foot on the rock.

The government finessed the naming question for its signature landmark by using both Uluru and Ayers Rock in its official name. Ulara—"howling"—the nearby town, is named for the calls of its wild dingoes.

I grew even more aware of the palimpsest of names after a student of tribal languages explained that the indigenous words for "soil" and "soul," "heart" and "homeland," "earth" and "spirit" are all the same. The Koori languages recognize no difference between themselves and the earth they come from.

But many tribal languages have a special word to describe looking out from beneath a sheltering overhang and connecting deeply with the land. Sometimes lightheartedly translated as "veranda-ing," it seems to combine contentment, contemplation, a sense of ownership, and an energetic connection unique to Koori people. Veranda-ing, elders gaze over the landscape, checking to see that all is well, and when necessary, restoring energetic balance.

For me, there's a multi-layered message about the power of naming something that goes beyond the respectful courtesy of learning to identify places, creatures, shrubs, and flowers. Rumpelstiltskin says that being able to name someone (or something) means you're no longer controlled by its mystery. To name, to identify, brings something to consciousness—the first step toward transformation. I think about domestic violence, once considered a woman's personal shame instead of a punishable crime with serious consequences, and how Betty Friedan helped launch the second wave of feminism by writing about the dissatisfaction that had no name. Naming has a resonating power; naming touches on truth, lets you share its personal mystery, take in a bit of it, be changed by the knowing.

I love the incantory resonance of exotic names, like the way Yackandandah and Wolongong feel in my mouth. The name galah tells me as much about the carefree nature of these pink and gray parrot cousins as their comical fluff-up topknots. I'm amused that the same flower that escaped from a garden to cloak countless hillsides in rich purple is called either "Salvation Jane" or "Patterson's Curse," depending on whether you're in New South Wales or the state of Victoria.

The Orwellian power to whitewash with names—like calling a clear-cutting plan the Forest Preservation Act or dismissing the talking heads of Kata Tjuta by calling them "The Olgas"—gives me the willies, turning the sacred power of naming inside out.

Walking the brick-red dirt paths encircling the base of Uluru, my mind wandered in circles. The pattern may or may not have been the earth speaking to me, tumbling out bits of its own story, but I was relieved to be experiencing the desert directly, feeling its dusty dryness on my skin, hearing the scrunch of rock under my feet, smelling the hot-oven scent of parched grass and the tang of eucalyptus.

Judy, the biologist-turned hiker, returned euphoric after more than four hours of clambering up to the top of the Rock, displaying her trophy in an empty film canister: a freshwater shield shrimp, startlingly green and as big as a finger. "Dust-sized shrimp eggs blow about the desert at random, so a good rainstorm can create puddles of instant live shrimp soup," she explained excitedly. Certain that shield shrimp would have made an appearance after so much rain, she'd searched several pools on top of the Rock in vain and then overheard youngsters talking about a pool with "tadpoles." As a bona fide researcher, Judy had a special permit to gather specimens, while tourists doing the same thing would face steep fines.

Among the most primitive of living crustaceans, shield shrimp are one of more than thirty Aussie animals able to survive being completely dried out; their growth cycle may even require a period of desiccation, she explained. And I wondered if that might be true for me as well: that I also needed a bit of time completely dusty and dried out in order to continue growing.

Although I longed to listen to Uluru, our schedule demanded that we embark for Kata Tjuta. I tried consoling myself with the knowledge that, little more than a century ago, this short hour's drive had been a desert trek so arduous that it cost the lives of many a European exploring party.

As the talking stone heads played peek-a-boo around dunes of orange-red soil, I was oppressed by the utter absence of water. No springs or standing pools softened the rockscape as they had at Uluru. A patina of desert varnish polished the stone surfaces smooth in red hues that shifted from mahogany to bleached orange with the angle of the sun. Along the path, a few wattles bravely raised golden orange puffs, but nary a tree to offer a smidgen of shade. A single wildflower emerged from the handful of orange sand. Judy identified the purple blossom as a ptilotus, the only evidence of recent rainfall.

As we drew closer, what had appeared to be heads transformed themselves into huge, lush variations on primal female forms: breasts and buttocks and pregnant bellies lounged about in a Brobdingnagian sculpture garden. Wouldn't this be a natural for a women's sacred site? I wondered. Robin and I knew that any man who approaches a women's site—even accidentally—is breaking a significant taboo; he will often experience headaches or nausea if he accidentally strays too close. My teacher Joel said both Koori and white folks alike would be stricken by this protective energy; he saw it as one way that the earth cooperates in keeping sacred sites sacred. We scrutinized the men in our group for a sign of something out of the ordinary, but they seemed comfortable, and the sweltering landscape revealed not a whiff of female energy. Too obvious, we chuckled. Walking through the Valley of the Winds, we hoped in vain for a hint of breeze in the oven-like heat.

Oddly enough, the most comfortable spot at Kata Tjuta proved to be a block of toilets—strikingly beautiful and a positive blessing, compared to the over-taxed, thatch-roofed outhouses at the base of Uluru. Made of rammed earth, the structure perfectly matched the color and texture of its surroundings. Adobe-thick walls kept inside temperatures as cool as a pueblo while its ingenious architecture used temperature variations for natural air circulation. This rest stop used the latest technology, said the coach driver with patriotic pride — Clivus composting toilets, just like Quinn's, back in Beechworth. Robin and I gave five gold stars to the comfort station, the best facilities we'd seen in our cross-country trek, then looked at each other and began giggling. On second thought, maybe we were just a teensy bit off: The spectacularly cool, fresh, clean toilet facilities might well make it another sort of site sacred to modern traveling women.

■ ■ ■

At the crack of another cloudless, picturesque dawn, we reboarded the coach and drove through a gradually changing desert. Black and red parrots, pigeons, mynah birds, and honeyeaters competed with the drowsy monotony of riding along seemingly endless, straight red roads.

Then came a startling mirage moment: Palm trees swayed and camels moseyed along the base of barren rocky outcrops.

"These are not really palm trees, but cycads—trees that look like palms," said Judy, spotting grist for another onboard tutorial. "Actually, they're the most primitive form of conifers. In this youngish desert, rainfall is not very reliable, and the plants have not had time to specialize for the climate. Close relatives to their water-loving cousins on the coasts, they've just adapted to dryer conditions.

"Plants that have adapted include the mulga scrub and hundreds of varieties of acacias that have funnel shapes, to direct any trace of rain toward their roots," she continued.

"She-oaks have two kinds of roots: deep ones to reach water and a shallow root system close to the surface to gather any nutrients from the nitrogen-starved soil," she said gesturing toward a rapidly vanishing grove.

"We're like that, too," Robin whispered. "We have our deep roots—to all life, to our own families, whether they're chosen or acquired. Those keep us alive. The shallow roots are the new connections, like between us, that enliven and enrich, that help us expand outward, and gather whatever the world is offering us today."

"It's a nice metaphor," I replied, "and maybe that's why the older we get, the more funnel-like we become."

"Remember what John Flynn, of the Royal Flying Doctor Service, says: 'You are your friends.'"

Our botany lesson continued. "Here in the desert, with practically no available nitrogen, plants have two survival options: fix nitrogen themselves, like the wattles, cassias, and pea flowers, or host parasites in their roots to fix nitrogen for them. And some of those parasites make for interesting bush tucker—like the quandongs a few of us had enjoyed at Beltana."

"Funny—Judy didn't mention they were parasites when she offered us a taste," I whispered to Robin. "They were a treat."

"Another bush surprise," she replied. "Those tangy little fruits are sometimes called bush peaches—and I guess they're more like a fruit than a truffle, a mushroom, or anything else you might expect from a root parasite."

One night, after pitching our tent on the edge of yet another tiny settlement, Robin and I walked through an assortment of caravans that edged the campground. Lightning crackled through the clouds of storm on the darkening horizon, and, emboldened by the nearly crisp air, we ventured to the edge between the town and the desert beyond. Lulled into quiet companionability by the rocky crunch beneath our feet, we reached a place where the track forked and chose without thinking. Not a hundred yards down the path, my chest tightened and a sense of panic hit me like a wave. Scanning the surroundings, I saw only the soft desert darkness. Nothing to be afraid of, I told myself, listening as Robin's footfalls kept pace with mine. Suddenly we couldn't go any farther. It felt as if we'd bumped up against a vast wall of energy. A magnetic field? Some terrestrial black hole? Goose bumps climbed my arms and legs as, wordlessly, Robin and I turned and ran back to the fork in the road.

"Did you feel that?" she asked tentatively.

"Yes, but I couldn't begin to say what it was," I replied, equally uncertain. "I've heard that sometimes the Koori use energy fields to protect sacred sites. Do you suppose. . . ?"

"Whatever it is, it certainly doesn't want us around—and I'm not about to argue."

Half an hour later, back in the safety of our tent, we still shook.

■ ■ ■

Nearing Alice Springs, the earth began to tell another story. I was struck by the vast stretches of dry, sand-filled river floodways, dramatic witnesses to the Alice's eons-long dance with water. Sheltered by undulating shale-like cliffs, called the MacDonnell Range, Alice Springs straddles the confluence of three rivers—the Rowe, the Finke, and the Todd. These Australian rivers—benign-looking expanses of white, powder-fine sand lined with white-barked gum trees—held no water at the moment. But with just a little rain, they instantly transform into roaring torrents.

In Colorado, such flash floods dig canyons and arroyos deeper, but here bedrock is barely below the surface, so swollen rivers overflow their banks and stretch hundreds of feet wide. In the outback, bridges are expensive and rain infrequent so most desert folk live with the possibility of being cut off by floods or getting bogged in their gooey aftermath.

Acclaimed as the world's oldest, the fossil Fink River has held to the same course it created some four hundred fifty million years ago, not counting its occasional swellings. The Todd has a different claim to fame: It's the site of the hilarious

Henley-on-Todd regatta—a dry-land boat, foot, and camel race on the riverbed that provides justification for a week-long beer fest, Robin explained. Easter, 1989, marked the last big river flow.

These erratic rivers owe their existence to the encircling mountains, the MacDonnells and the Heavitree Range. Diminutive by Colorado standards—the highest mountain is only 4,954 feet—they still provide enough elevation to extract what little moisture the winds carry. In the center of this ultra-dry continent, Alice Springs may receive up to fifteen inches of rainfall a year—making it technically an arid zone, not a desert. But with an evaporation rate three times that of its rainfall, that's a distinction without much of a difference.

As we crossed the Hugh River following a flat and empty brick-red road, Maurie, the geologist, struggled unsuccessfully to explain the origin of the low, rolling hills breaking the horizon line. Some inexplicable forces came into play to create the MacDonnell Range, defying most known principles of geology. There's no satisfactory geophysical explanation of what forces can create a mountain range smack in the midst of a stable continent.

Also, at roughly the same time, some three hundred fifty million years ago, a sort of twisting took place, rotating a block of the earth's crust clockwise around a pivot point in the Tanami Desert, two hundred fifty miles to the northwest. This gigantic kneading not only squeezed up Australia's longest mountain chain but also opened up a vast depression called the Kimberley Trough in Western Australia. Dating the rocks, geologists can provide a timeline for these movements but no explanation.

"Big Earth Medicine is alive in this part of the world," Robin said.

"The science types hate it when the simplest, most rational, explanation is 'unknown forces.'" I laughed. "Call it medicine or call it magic, I'm sure the Koori people have a story that explains all this."

■ ■ ■

Jean had organized this trip to return to the land of her childhood. She had grown up with the tribal people near Alice Springs while her father worked for the Flying Doctor Service. To prepare us for visiting Hermannsburg, the country's first Aboriginal reservation and still the largest, she began with a bit of history. "Years ago, when the blacks were cast out of the white community, the government decided to follow the U.S. model for dealing with Native Americans; they isolated them on reservations, always located on the poorest land, some distance from towns and cities."

Before she'd finished, a voice in the back of the bus began some barely audible grumbling, complaining about wasting our time traveling to a place "filled with dead cars and Abos." The word shocked me as much as hearing someone say "nigger," but Jean didn't miss a beat.

"Sometimes people complain that the reservations are littered with junk," she continued, seizing the teachable moment; "but please remember that before the Europeans arrived, anything a native discarded looked natural on the landscape—a broken digging stick or a rock that didn't crack into the right shape. When you know how to look, you can find half-completed implements just about anywhere," she said, reaching down to retrieve a pinkish-gray stone a few feet from where she stood.

"I can't tell what this was supposed to be, but you can see someone knapped a ridge along one side of this stone," she said, holding up the newly found relic for all to see, then passing it around the encircling group. "Any trash you may see on the reservation comes from our way of life, not theirs. We're the ones who've created the non-biodegradable plastic that's become rubbish. And the Aborigines aren't the only ones who've ringed their towns with junker cars and mountains of dead tires."

"After growing up with the Aborigines, Jean loves and respects them," Robin whispered as we returned to our seats. "But prejudice against them is still so strong, especially as you head north. It's interesting to see Jean seize any opportunity to counteract people's preconceived ideas."

I tried to imagine living where everything you used was simply part of the landscape and couldn't help wondering just how dismal Hermannsburg would prove to be.

As we broke for afternoon tea, Jean sat down with us and asked, "Was I too harsh?" Robin and I exchanged puzzled glances. Oblivious to our response, or lack of it, she continued: "I know I should have been more gentle, less lecture-y. Most of the grumblers are just my neighbors—poor old retired dairy farmers who've soaked up this country's prejudice like stale bread in a bowl of milk. They're interested in the Doctor Service, not native culture. But I can't help it. Whenever I hear 'What can you expect from Abos?' I lose my cool. It's frustrating, in this day and age, to still be bumping up against that kind of prejudice, that close-mindedness."

"That's one of the worst parts of living in a country town for me, too," Robin agreed.

Seated companionably around a picnic table, both women seemed eager to talk about this touchy subject, so I plunged ahead. "So far, I haven't seen any serious prejudice in Australia —although occasional incidents show up in the newspaper. I want to understand what fuels this anti-native prejudice, but I don't know much about its history. Is it racial prejudice? The simple fear of 'the other' or something else? Is there a history of black slavery?"

"No, not slavery—at least in the sense of what you had in America. Interestingly, some of the northern tribes were once slaveholders themselves. But there is the prejudice against dark-skinned people—or any people who look different—and a legacy of cultural misunderstanding dating back to first contact, when the Europeans first arrived," Jean said.

"Maybe it's cultural, maybe it's racial, but it seems like many whites have always held the Aborigines in contempt. Some people say it's because they didn't put up a huge fight when the Europeans first arrived," Robin said.

"True. They didn't offer any resistance. They took a wait-and-see attitude toward the newcomers, and the Europeans interpreted that as cowardice," Jean added. "But it's also more subtle than that. Let's see, where to start?"

Robin joined her in full-on teacher mode: "First of all, you need to know that when an Aborigine dies, his skin turns an ashy white. So, when the Europeans first landed, the natives thought these bizarre strangers had just drifted in from the world of the dead."

"They took a look at Captain Cook and his men and decided they must be spirit visitors on some important mission. Or long-dead ancestors returning with some important message," Jean said.

They conjured up quite an image: naked dark men, decorated with daubs of colored mud, feathers, and the occasional cloak or penis sheath, gawking at a bunch of British redcoats trying to assemble in formation and not gawk back, each scaring the other half-silly.

"It must have felt incredibly spooky," I said, remembering Joel telling me that sometimes the Koori dead were placed in canoes and floated out to sea. "A bit like the sea giving up its dead—not as bodies, but as live, walking strangers who talked an alien language. Sounds like the plot of some strange time-travel movie."

"There was some debate among the elders about whether the European intruders were actually human. Many of the Brits were uniformed soldiers—which must have looked especially bizarre to folks unaccustomed to any sort of body covering," Jean said. "Some thought these spirit-beings had acquired hard shells, like beetles or crabs. According to legend, one night a bold Koori peered through a peephole and watched the soldiers undress, then spread the word that their rigid coverings came off to reveal pale but recognizable human males."

"I remember reading that the redcoats were welcomed by the natives, who thought they were the dead returned to life; the soldiers regarded the natives as hopelessly stupid," Robin offered.

"Mostly, the natives feigned a sort of nonchalance, waiting for these mysterious gubbas to reveal their purpose. They regarded the newcomers like slightly retarded little brothers: oddballs who had been away from real human companionship so long that they didn't remember how to talk or know how to behave properly. They didn't share. They fought among themselves. They even killed each other.

"And the most extraordinary, most remarkable thing of all," said Jean, "was that they were all men. There wasn't a woman among them.

"Now I've gone full-on lecture-y," she laughed as she stood up. "Wish I'd figured out earlier what kind of a group we have. I would have planned to take the whole lot to the Strehlow Center and saved my breath. But now we'd all better get some sleep. We're locked into this itinerary that includes some major sightseeing." She nodded goodnight.

"The Strehlow Center?" Robin and I grasped that same fragment simultaneously. We knew where we'd head on our first free day in Alice Springs.

And the center didn't disappoint. An attractive sandstone colored building, the center was devoted to the research begun by an early settler, Willliam Strehlow, whose deep affection for Aboriginal culture was reflected in the artifacts on display, the tasteful choices for sale in the museum's store and, most beautifully, in a slide show. Fading from the image of a tribal elder to a kangaroo, merging dot paintings and the landscape to the sounds of click sticks and didgeridoos, it was a presentation that brought Koori culture to life and reduced us both to tears.

■ ■ ■

I was prepared for Hermannsburg to be bleak. What I wasn't prepared for was the way the settlement was dominated by a church, nor for the pre-sermon-like hush that pervaded the whole place.

I'd envisioned something like Taos Pueblo, where the energy of muted magic still hums beneath the dry, dusty surface. Instead, the old wooden structures, the tin-roofed buildings, the grim dormitories, and the fierce chapel exuded an air of hopelessness.

This settlement was the home of Albert Namatjira, a famous Aboriginal artist who had easily mastered the European landscape tradition to portray the haunting desert luminance of the ghost gum trees and pink-purple hills. Robin was eager to see his haunts.

Trying not to be too obtrusively tourist-like, I walked among the bleached buildings, seeking a sense of the artist, a trace of Namatjira's impact among dusty footpaths where even the afternoon bees buzzed lazily. The settlement had the energy of a graveyard, one that held the remnants of a spiritual clash between the Christians, who believed they were saving the ignorant Heathen, and the quiet, semi-secret Koori, whose gentle Earth connections had sustained them through millennia. No energy, no spirit, no magic, just incredibly poor people trying to survive in a place that had long ago stripped away their dignity and challenged the very roots of their culture.

I had no idea about the violence used against these people. I only sensed its threatening presence. And felt shamed by it. For the rednecks in our group, Hermannsburg provided something new to criticize, grumbling about the "slow-moving," "lazy," and "shiftless," Aborigines they'd observed shuffling along the dusty tracks of the settlement.

Judy marshaled her biological knowledge to their defense. "These are desert people, adapted to living in the heat. If you rush around in this heat, you risk death. Too much activity and you lose more moisture through sweat than your body can replenish. It's a hard lesson for white people, who tend to think that faster is better.

"Studies have been done about water-holding frogs. Have you ever seen an Aborigine dig out a frog? She'll take her stick and slowly begin to scrape a hole, stop and rest, then dig a little bit more. It might take half the day to dig all the way down to the frog.

"A white person goes after a frog like a little rat terrier—digging frantically. And what researchers found was that, by rushing, you lost more moisture than the frog contained."

Others began pressing Judy for details of the study; I, boggling at the idea of a water-holding frog, turned to Robin. "How do you get water out of a frog? You can't milk it."

"You just put the frog in your mouth and suck on it gently. They don't really give up that much water, maybe a quarter of a cup. Just enough to take the edge off your thirst."

"You've tried it? You've sucked water out of a frog?"

"It tastes a bit muddy. Or froggy. Traditionally, you're supposed to put the frog back in its hole with a prayer of thanks—which seems only fair. If you're lost in the desert, knowing how to spot where a frog's dug in can make all the difference"

"I suppose you've eaten witchiti grubs, too?"

"Not raw," she recoiled. "But roasted, they taste a lot like peanut butter."

I just adored that woman.

■ ■ ■

Next up: Palm Valley.

"Are you ready for a day of unintentional aerobics?" asked Derek, the cheerful cook-driver-guide, his jeep lurching along a dry, sandy riverbed mined with rocks. Lured by the image of an oasis, Robin and I had joined a half dozen adventuresome visitors for the Palm Valley day trip, but so far we'd just seen sand, sand, and more sand. As we reached the Finke Gorge, the track widened to detour around puddles and wet places that can bog a vehicle just like quicksand.

"Right here a Land Rover was bogged for five weeks," said Derek, with a maniac cheeriness that made it impossible for me to figure out if he were indulging in a good yarn or simply recounting improbable Aussie facts. He took a sharp right turn off the riverbed into a canyon. Bouncing over boulders approaching the size of Volkswagens, Derek hardly paused in his narrative as he pointed to a cave above a ranger station, steering single-handed. "That ranger was glad enough for that cave when the floods raged through their house. He and the whole family were trapped up there for three days."

"You mean flood waters topped this bluffy outcrop? It must be three hundred feet high," said Robin, ignoring the niceties of metric conversion.

"Yup. A fair dinkum flood it was," he grinned, relishing the joy of surviving any adversity that Mother Nature threw his way.

As we bounced along the Marpa Track, a small herd of brumbies—wild horses—galloped by. Four legs instead of four wheels seemed far more appropriate to this tooth-rattling terrain. I felt relieved when he pulled to a stop, leaped out, opened the passenger door with a flourish. "Take all the time you want to enjoy Palm Valley, but mind the water. I wouldn't be drinking it—or stepping in it."

A chameleon-sized lizard greeted me, dancing from one foot to the other, celebrating the intense heat of the sizzling rock beneath his scaly toes. Behind him, the valley opened like a huge cleft in the desert floor. One side was a gentle hill, the other rose to a steep, rocky cliff bursting with short, palm-like cycads. Granite boulders and sandstone slabs lay jumbled on the valley floor, forming rough bridges amid puddles and pools of water that teemed with strange reeds and bulrushes.

What struck me most about Palm Valley was the sound, a gentle, chattering murmur from the bulrushes and palm fronds. Clicking and swaying, thousands of palm trees stretched straight up, reaching more than thirty feet above the broad valley floor. I instantly fell under the spell of these stately, elegant anachronisms.

"This stand of *Livistona mariae* palms is a relic of a time some ten thousand years ago when a wetter Australia supported palm forests through much of its interior," said Derek, reading from a leaflet. "As the continent's climate slowly dried, the palms retreated, leaving behind this small band of survivors. They were protected from desert wildfires by the high valley walls, and these porous rocks gathered dew and provided just enough seepage to sustain the trees. The nearest other stand of *Livistona* is some six hundred miles northeast, in a far more appropriate tropical rain forest. This is a spectacular botanical refuge that protects more than three hundred other plant species, many quite rare."

Touching their rough bark and feeling the massive, mat-like root systems of a few that had toppled over did nothing to change the improbable magic of a hidden oasis of stately palms amid a scorching desert.

Crunchy from the sand and dryness, and stupefied by the heat of a day in the desert, we returned to our accommodations —a backpackers' hostel most notable for its breakfast offerings of canned spaghetti or baked beans on toast.

"I thought such fare existed only in British novels," I laughed.

"It's not half bad," said Robin, "and it's sustained generations of poor but determined British students, wherever they find themselves."

■ ■ ■

While I found the hidden world of Palm Valley awesome —in the original sense of the word—geologists and biologists consider Kings Canyon of more scientific significance. My assignment was for *Earth Magazine,* so the canyon, notched into the westernmost mountains of the George Gill Range, was a must. I'd be writing for serious rock lovers who might never experience these ancient formations themselves and wondered what details would bring this trip to life. We arrived on a hot and sunny day, with a few tiny clouds hanging high in the sky. Camouflaged with white-barked gum trees and cypress pines, the deceptively low-key canyon entrance gave no hint that within lay extravagant cliffs and domes of weathered sandstone that loomed like so many giant Navajo hogans. Towering cliffs of layered red sandstone made the deep canyon feel lopsided. Desert vegetation demonstrated its endurance, sprouting from smidgens of sand trapped in rocky fractures.

Robin chose to hike along the top of the canyon-rimming cliffs, while I opted for the low road, an easy path along the canyon floor, walled on one side by two-hundred-foot-high stacks of sandstone so brittle that the stone practically sheared off when you looked at it. The track ended at a grove where, thanks to Judy's coaching, I could identify cycad palms, native figs, and river red gums—a paltry fraction of the different plants sheltered by the towering walls and watered by seepage from the canyon's cracks and fissures.

For Maurie, the geologist, this was sandstone heaven. "The lower, rubbley part of the cliff face is Carmichael sandstone, deposited some four hundred forty million years ago," he said, thrilled by the scenic evidence of the earth's restless churning. "Over that, the almost vertical face is Mereenie sandstone. The sand was deposited by a long-vanished river some three hundred sixty million years ago."

Crimped and folded like some enormous puff pastry crust, this layered sandstone was then fractured in place by whatever mysterious geological whirls and pivots had lifted up the MacDonnell Range, he said. Slabs of younger, honey-hued sandstone were scattered on the valley floor.

Examining one of those sparkly, quartz-rich rocks more closely, I could hardly believe my eyes—the unmistakable pattern of fossil ripple marks was preserved on the rock's surface.

Extracting lunch from my backpack, I sat down near the sandstone slabs, struggling to make discovering these fossilized marks of water into a sort of emotional or intellectual high point. Elation eluded me. The chatter of the other coach passengers echoed through the canyon created a low-level irritation; I couldn't feel the subtle hum of the earth. I felt cheated.

Feeling ever so sorry for myself, I grew pissy and grouchy, longing for the everyday life I'd nicely constructed to support the notion that I was a patient, tolerant, accepting person. Living alone insulated me from most mundane travel-induced trials like tedium, mediocre food, and, most of all, the company of people I'd never seek out. My snobbish intolerance yowled up, fed by every thoughtless comment and vapid observation—mine and others—I'd endured so far on this journey. How did some people manage to swim untouched through these social encounters like so many pilot fish?

I missed Robin, who'd opted for the other hike, longing to see if she, too, was finding the journey a bit maddening.

"Interesting how the canyon brought your shadow to the surface," she observed. "Up on the rim, I left the others and found myself listening to quarrelsome voices, too. But they seemed to be coming from the rocks. I'm betting you connected to the earth's energy after all—and it just wasn't what you expected. We've learned a lot about the geology of this place, but nothing about what people did here. Maybe battles were fought or people were murdered here."

■ ■ ■

On a day off from planned excursions, I decided to search for Aboriginal art among the numerous galleries of Alice Springs. Wandering among the dot paintings and more familiar landscapes of dusty rivers lined with stately white-barked gum trees, I heard someone begin playing a didgeridoo, first trying one, then another, filling the gallery with rich base notes, bird-like chirps, animal calls, and undulating whistles. Glancing around, I saw a fellow with long, sun-bleached hair tied back with a thong, a leather hat, and leather vest over his naked chest, as if he'd wandered in from some Crocodile Dundee look-alike contest, trying out some of the gallery's stock of elaborately decorated didjs. As this process was repeated in the next gallery and the next, I couldn't help smiling. I'd peruse the artworks, hoping for something I could afford to take home, while the leather-clad stranger offered brief, impromptu concerts. After half a dozen galleries, there seemed no point in trying to contain my curiosity.

"You're obviously not looking for a souvenir. You certainly get quite an array of sounds out of those. What sort of quality are you looking for?" I asked.

"I'm a musician. Play in a bit of a knock-about band, and while we're here, I thought I'd find me a didj with a nice bass voice. It's nice to have a lot to choose from," he replied. "Usually the thicker ones have a deeper tone. And the length has something to do with it, too. Here. Listen to this one," he said, skillfully evoking a range of chirps, whoops, and haunting didj sounds.

"What sort of music do you play?" I asked.

"We're a bit of a bush band. Dancing, tap-your-toes tunes. You know, the popular stuff. We get a lot of gigs around town," he said, half-apologizing.

"Not your cup of tea? Well, what sort of music do you enjoy playing?" I asked.

"What I really love is hard to explain. It's authentic. Rich. Soulful—a lot like the CD that's playing right now."

"It's one of my favorites, too," said the woman behind the counter, easily joining the conversation of the only customers she had in her gallery. "It's the most listenable of all the Aboriginal music I've heard—and I hear Aboriginal music all the time" she said, nodding toward the CDs behind her counter.

"I know this by heart. It's called 'Track to Bumbliwa,' the work of two musicians in Boulder, Colorado, where I come from. Although I think they recorded some of the didj here in Australia," I said. As I flowed back in time to a little cinder-block art gallery full of Aboriginal women's dot paintings, then to the gallery in Alice Springs, something came full circle.

■ ■ ■

Nothing could change the fact that more than two thousand miles of hard desert driving lay ahead, however. Far too quickly we were back in the coach heading through towering termite nests standing snaggletoothed across the red desert floor, heading north. We had no idea that Robin's moment of completion, equally unexpected but far more painful, lay ahead.

When we stopped for a day in Curdimurka, Robin and I went walking to stretch our legs, get a close-up sense of the odd little mining town, find a nice café, and enjoy a morning coffee. Spotting a likely looking shop that evoked the Beechworth Bakery, I headed toward the door just as Robin started to crumple onto the footpath.

"What's wrong?" I asked, grabbing my falling companion.

"I turned my ankle. Didn't see that little hump of concrete there," she said, her face white with pain.

"Take a minute to catch your breath and recover a bit. You look like you're in shock," I said as she struggled to regain her feet.

"I'm afraid I've done myself some real damage," she said, tears welling up in her eyes. "I think I've sprained or broken something. Dammit!"

"Let's head back to the motel. It's not far. Someone there will know where we can go for help," I said, holding up her suddenly small body.

"How clumsy! I can't believe I wasn't watching my step," she grumbled, ignoring my reassurances that all would be well. The motel clerk instantly summoned an ambulance.

"Now this is a whole different trip," she joked as attendants strapped her onto a gurney. "What will this mean for the rest of our journey?" By this time Robin was not only in serious pain but wildly self-conscious about being the center of attention for the growing crowd of curious gawkers drawn by the flashing emergency lights.

"Don't worry about anything. Just take care of yourself. I'll come see you as soon as I can," I said, giving her a big hug as she was loaded into the ambulance.

A whole day passed and a second one was descending into ruddy twilight when the word came that Robin was ready for a visitor.

Entering her room filled with nervous caution, I was surprised to see her sitting up in the hospital bed looking positively radiant.

"Remember what Jung said—that there are no accidents?" she asked, her dark eyes dancing with excitement.

"You arranged to have a different kind of trip?"

"Exactly! she laughed. "But not in the way you might be thinking. There's a story I haven't told you that begins more than twenty years ago when my sister, Evelyn, living the role of the perfect vicar's daughter in rural Lancaster, suddenly found herself pregnant. No one raised an eyebrow when she decided to visit me, living at an altogether convenient distance away, here in Australia."

"So you and Evelyn hatched this plan...?"

"Not at all. It was her plan entirely, although she told me about it. She came to Curdimurka, had the baby, gave it up for adoption, and returned to England."

"She never even came to see you?"

"No, she couldn't afford to travel all the way down to Victoria. To this day, I'm still not sure where she got the money for her passage. And I was a farmer's wife, too poor, and too busy with three small sons, to visit her.

"But if there were any hospital in all of Australia that I would like to be in—this is it," she said, glancing around the room with a satisfied smile. "This is where her baby was born. Evelyn never talked about it. So a huge, traumatic part of my sister's life was just a vacant space. Although I knew the bare bones, the idea of my making a sort of pilgrimage or fact-finding mission to Curdimurka always seemed odd. What would I look for? Who would I talk to? But now, here, like this..." she said waving her hand to encompass her bed, the room, the whole clinic.

"Your curiosity is satisfied?"

"More than I ever dreamed. I even found one of the nursing sisters who was working here back then. She remembered Evelyn."

"Well, isn't that extraordinary! Amazing that she's still here and remembered a maternity case ages ago!"

"Actually it's probably not that surprising. I'll wager there aren't many unwed mothers from Lancashire who found their way here and then gave their babies up for adoption."

"I hadn't thought about that."

In such a tiny hospital, probably less than fifty beds, it was easy to imagine the nursing sisters buzzing about anything even remotely out of the ordinary.

"Did you ever try to find out what happened to the baby?"

Robin shook her head. "We don't even know if it was a boy or a girl. Somehow Evelyn thought not knowing would make it all less painful. And since this was a very tender subject for her, I couldn't go poking about and asking questions without her permission. That would be an awful violation of her trust. So I tried to convince myself that if she didn't need to know, why should I? But I still felt something strangely unfulfilled. Until now, when I found all my questions answered by accident." She glowed with satisfaction

When Robin was released from the hospital, complete with crutches and cast, she needed the long, flat seat at the back of the coach to stretch out on as our road trip resumed. If I sat in back with her, the motion and fumes threatened to trigger a migraine. Our special needs forced a separation that changed the trip. It became an exercise in coping with the worst kind of alone—surrounded by indifferent people—as we wended our way back to Victoria.

Reading brought on headaches and motion sickness. Spending time "inside my body," I tended to focus on small-scale discomforts: the abrasive upholstery against the back of my knees, the itch of random bug bites on my arms or ankles, the desert tautness of the skin on my face, how crunched and confined I felt. The limited range of motion possible in a bus seat became a kind of prison.

I remembered the old joke about flying being long stretches of boredom interrupted by moments of sheer terror; the coach tour was proving to be long stretches of tedium, interrupted by bits of enjoyment or aggravation. After weeks of driving, Judy, Maurie, and Jean seemed to succumb to the hypnotic lassitude of endless miles of sameness.

With notably less frequency, Judy made the coach driver stop so she could dash out and gather a few plants or the occasional wildflowers to pass around as we traveled.

But Maurie, the geologist, grew excited as signs said we were nearing the Henbury Craters—"ginormous" double bull's-eyes created ages ago when thirteen meteorites slammed into the desert floor. Like rocks hitting a windscreen, the meteorites sprayed out circles of glassy shocked quartz. "Some of the bands are miles across—a key to the staggering size of the meteorites," he said, turning to me in hopes I'd share his enthusiasm.

"I'll bet there are some amazing Koori creation stories about those. Do you know any? Should we go to see them?" I asked.

He thought a moment, then shook his head. "Well, actually I guess you'd have to be a geologist to appreciate what you're looking at. Otherwise they're just rocks around gigantic depressions in the desert floor," he replied.

I found his honesty touching. We decided to skip the craters.

Cattle munching the mulga scrub posed for some poster on the perils of overgrazing, mindlessly resisting the palpable power of the desert that seemed more than the sum of heat, wind, and dryness. As I noticed more and more dead kangaroos alongside the road, I began sensing a kind of unfocused malevolence.

"Is there something particularly lethal to kangaroos hereabouts?" I asked.

"Paved roads can provide a kind of drainage, so that the areas right along the edge get a bit more moisture and produce a tiny bit more forage," Judy explained. "And grazing right next to the road, they're more vulnerable to passing vehicles."

"That's only part of it," Jean added. "Things are wilder, more like the wild frontier, up here in the Northern Territory. You've seen those trucks with a row of lights mounted on top? They're shooting rigs. They go out at night and make the roos freeze with fright with their bright lights, then shoot 'em like fish in a barrel. Sometimes they go after them with baseball bats. They consider it fun to chase down kangaroos with a truck."

"They're obviously not hunting for food," I said, shocked by the idea of bashing these charming, doe-eyed creatures.

"It's a shame, but they just leave it all to go to waste. A native would consider a kangaroo a feast."

Looking out the window, I was transported back to the High Plains, overwhelmed with sadness and rage from watching the senseless slaughter of buffalo, wishing I had Jilba's courage to halt the coach, to make offerings for the animals' spirits.

Instead, I moved between then and now, grieving in silence.

The road became more of a by-guess-and-by-gosh proposition. Choosing the flattest-looking path across the pounded red sand and threading our way through muddy patches that could bog us down, we made slow progress. At one point a four-foot-long goanna seemed to be making better time than we were. Other times the driver had to swing wide at the approach of monstrous road trains—gargantuan trucks pulling three or four fully loaded trailers. Hauling along at breakneck speed, choosing a path as they go, the road trains spew out glass-shattering boulders with a hundred churning wheels.

A bit crazy from the passive numbingness of staring out the coach windows and the sad spectacle of murdered kangaroos, I realized I had neither the stamina nor the skills for the desert life. Even the more muted experiences of this trip would have been too much without Robin providing my emotional base. We couldn't connect with our fellow travelers, much less the tribal people, which left me with an odd feeling. Was it a sense of superiority, a recognition that I wasn't like them—and glad of it? A bit of snootiness about the tiny settlements? Enormously glad, or relieved, that the Red Centre is not my life? Amazed at those who choose the rough life of tiny desert settlements? I felt no tug toward the rugged independence, no envy of those content with educating their children by radio lessons from the School of the Air, or awe for those who thrived on medical care from the Flying Doctor Service, although I watched many of the Australians go all misty-eyed about it. Funny, but it was easier to feel the appeal of the Aboriginal tribal existence than the pull of William Creek or Urandangi, Quamby, or Mount Isa.

Feeling both sadness and relief, I dozed, snuggling into the stifling protection of the lumbering cocoon of a coach humming along the Matilda Highway, still nearly a thousand miles from Beechworth and some immeasurable distance from home.

The trip to the Centre felt like a vast, multi-layered metaphor, one I struggled to decipher.

Epilogue: Return Again

At the train station, Robin's son awaited our arrival. "How did you enjoy your whole trip?" he asked. "I'm glad I did it—but I wouldn't want to do it again," she replied; her summary echoed my feelings, too. While Robin recounted some highlights of the journey, I sat in the backseat, relishing the time alone, anticipating the chance to walk Beechworth's familiar footpaths, to let my feet move while my mind roamed, looking for the patterns, the lessons. No dreams had come to guide me during the journey in the land of the Dreaming. And then I remembered how dreams often vanish when your waking life becomes dream-like.

The languorous process of sifting my experiences and sorting my memories would haunt me for years, while, in humbling contrast, Robin had her photos from our trip printed, captioned, and mounted in albums within a fortnight.

When they dropped me off at Finch Street, I was disappointed that my flat was empty and no one was in the workshop. Feeling vaguely silly, I realized I longed for some kind of a welcome, a sense that I'd been missed, to know someone noticed my absence, to confirm that I hadn't simply awakened from a dream.

Maybe Quinn's working on the new lace shop, I thought, dropping my bags and heading to the center of town, past gardens and hedges sprouting new spring growth in jaunty hues of green and red.

On Ford Street, a woman I barely knew exclaimed, "You're back from the desert!" Smiling vaguely as I recognized her face, I marveled that she even knew about my trip, momentarily forgetting the power of small-town gossip.

"I'm sure your trip was fabulous," she continued, not bothering to pause for a response. "You wouldn't dare come back from a trip to the Centre and say you didn't enjoy it. No Aussie would tolerate that."

"It was amazing," I managed, ordinary words growing thick on my tongue. I felt as numb and dull-witted as when I'd returned from working in Calcutta during monsoon season.

Her comment made me realize that I'd bumbled into a sort of cultural sacrament: The Red Centre is sacred heartland to Australians, natives, and newcomers, white and black; all vowed that they would visit the desert someday. I hadn't realized the significance of all the stories of people inexplicably drawn to the Red Centre, of families who took their kids out of school for six months, a year, or more, so they could experience the desert interior together. The pull of the land is so strong, its power so compelling that few remain untouched by it; and I myself was simply stunned.

What did it mean, to stay with the power of the Dreaming, I wondered, as my feet kept me on the search for Quinn. Was there a way to stay in the bardo between taking a journey and returning to life's dailyness long enough for me to sort out my experiences and begin to decode the lessons that whispered in my ears?

When I found Quinn amidst the sawdust of his current project, he swept me up in a gratifying hug. "Good to see you back," he said. "Glad you did it?"

I nodded, still struggling for words to wrap around the tumble of feelings and experiences.

"While you were on your journey, I began to realize that soon you'll be gone again, heading back to the old U.S. of A. Hard to believe the time's gone by so quickly," he said amiably.

The next big return. Funny, that had fled my mind, too. Would I recover from this dose of culture shock before taking on the struggles of re-entry? Silent and dumbstruck, I saw Tia breezing into the construction zone of the soon-to-be lace shop.

"I was hoping to see you today," she exclaimed, opening her arms for an embrace, then, with a practiced pause to brush him free of bits of wood and sawdust, she hugged Quinn as well. "The boy's got so much work to do, he forgot his lunch," she smiled, brandishing a brown paper bag. "But I'm free. Let's nick into the Parlor and Pantry and have a bit of tea, and I'll catch you up with our news."

Tea in Australia is an elastic notion that expands to include everything from a quick "cuppa" to a light mid-morning snack, an afternoon break, or a casual evening meal, depending on the time of day. But context is all. For Tia, a chance to have tea at the Parlor and Pantry meant an opportunity to indulge in some special treat; the talented chef offered a constantly changing assortment of cream scones, fruited sponges, and delicately frosted layer cakes that unfailingly prompted an agony of delighted indecision. I needed no urging to join her in celebrating tasting.

Once we declared we'd share bites, it was a bit easier for me to settle on a lemon tart and for Tia to choose a kiwi and blueberry concoction. Tia radiated excitement but waited until we took our seats at a table overlooking Camp Street, then hugged my arm. "We just found out that Logan will be leaving, going back to live with his mother and stepfather, and Quinn's daughter, Morgan, will be coming to stay with us for a school term. And your time here seems to be moving so fast you'll be leaving before any of us really notices. So our little family circle will be shifting again."

"One door closes and another one opens, as they say," I answered, "but this seems to be a bit of a revolving door for you—first me, then Logan, and now Morgan."

"Morgan's not the unknown quantity you were when you arrived," Tia said with a smile. "I guess I'm a little afraid, just the teeniest bit apprehensive of changes in general. The biggest has been changing the kind of idyllic existence Quinn and I have been enjoying. No worries, both our kids gone, leaving just the two of us together in our little house in the country. In truth, there's no need to worry. It's mostly a reflex. I simply adore Morgan, and we've always gotten on."

"I was so impressed with her when we spent that weekend together in Adelaide. She's so mature, so capable, so self-assured for someone still in prep," I said, remembering her educational level wasn't exactly equivalent to high school.

"Yes, she's amazing. Knows the museums and galleries of Adelaide so well that I always use her as my guide whenever I visit the city. She just set out to master it—and did," said Tia, her affection for her stepdaughter opening like a flower in the sunshine. "I think she owes a lot of her poise and self-confidence to the Flying Fruit Fly Circus."

"Now there's a chapter I missed entirely," I laughed. "What is the Flying Fruit Fly Circus?"

"I think it began with a family or a troupe of Chinese acrobats, a group that spent its winters in Albury-Wodonga," she said, settling in for the full tale. "And somehow they began teaching little kids circus tricks: tumbling, mid-air summersaults, tightrope walking, flying trapeze stunts. Real circus performance things. And the kids loved them. Although they were littlies—from ages six or eight to maybe twelve years old—they practiced and practiced. All of them were working together toward the time when they put on a real circus show."

"It makes sense, to learn those tricks when you're young, limber, and fearless," I said. "I always thought you practically had to be born into a circus family to be able to do that stuff."

"Learning to tightrope walk or do trapeze stunts before you hit puberty is an amazing confidence-builder. Plus, there's something special that comes from being a part of professional-quality performances," she bubbled.

"I can't imagine what that must feel like."

"You won't be surprised to know that Quinn thought the Flying Fruit Flies would be important for Morgan. He was the one who got up early every morning for ages and drove her to Wodonga to practice."

"Did Logan join the circus, too, when he reached that age?"

"No. I'm not sure why. Maybe because it was so clearly identified as his big sister's thing. But much of this was before Quinn and I got together."

And, of course, years before I arrived here, I thought, feeling the now-familiar pang at yet another important part of my brother's life I'd missed. After nearly a year of feeling re-connected with him, I was teased by a vague sense that the new life he'd created down under, the connections among his accepting and loving little Australian family, offered a kind of Rosetta stone that could help me decipher what was missing in my own life. But I had no idea where to go with that notion. Instead, I fell back into my writer's reflexes:

What a brilliant idea—using circus skills to teach kids self-confidence, I thought, especially when it helped create the intelligent, resourceful, and utterly competent young adult like my niece, Morgan. Was it an idea worth sharing? Were the results reproducible? Had anyone done a follow-up study, to track Flying Fruit Fly "graduates" to determine the impact of their experience, I wondered, spinning off the beginnings of researching a magazine piece about the merits of circus performance as a character-building experience.

I'd felt a similar surge when I found out that inmates in the Beechworth prison trained seeing-eye dogs; I fell in love with the win-win idea. Inmates can transform days of endless monotony with a combination of outdoor exercise and meaningful purpose, gain a chance to experience the healing power of canine love while making a positive contribution to society, I exulted. What a way to learn, gently and powerfully, about the impact of their actions. Working with animals is a true heart opener, which also helps make a good story.

But was this whole journey about finding topics to write about?

Story ideas were simply my own kind of mirage—engaging diversions that led me away from facing the fact that I'd soon be leaving. No magazine article could keep me linked into daily life with Quinn and his family, or strengthen my ties to Robin, or help sustain the small circle of women slowly coalescing in Beechworth. My fear was that once I returned to my familiar Boulder routine, my experiences would fade away like the discolored photos of my childhood. What could I bring back to prevent that stealthy creep of amnesia? Could I find the lesson, the moral to the story, the point?

Preparing to leave included saying farewell to Ingram's Rock, that special little place that spoke to my heart. The walking track was carved with little rivulets from the rain as I neared the donkey, Jenny, grazing in her field. I scratched the ear she offered, and she nuzzled for a handful of fresh-picked grass. Who had introduced me to Jenny, told me her name? Was it Logan? Quinn? Someone I'd met along the pathway? Already memories were fading, I realized with a whiff of panic.

Open your heart and you're changed forever. But what tugged at my heart that moment—the soft squish of mud on the now-familiar track, the tang of wet eucalyptus in the air, the resignation in the eyes of a donkey who'd been all but forgotten by the family that once doted on her?

Maybe standing on Ingram's Rock would tell me. Suddenly I was filled with a yearning rush to be there, as anxious as if I were late for a lover's tryst. I hurried past the pea-flowered wattles, some small, intensely blue-violet flowers, those blooming in vivid yellow and red, and other flowers I recognized as the cousin to the pea that my grandma called "bacon & eggs." Suddenly a magpie dive-bombed for my head. Heart pounding, I frantically waved my hands over my head, yelling "Stop! Stop!"—the instinctive response to the aerial assaults of a magpie. I flailed about until she finally realized I posed no threat to her nest and let me pass. No harm done, being ambushed by five pounds of sharp-beaked maternal fury. No deep significance. Just chalk up another Australian experience.

Entering the grove of white-barked trees, my breathing calmed, and I approached the low granite outcropping, picking my way across the rivulets flowing down the rock face. Stepping into the clearing where the humming green hills stretched out below, I looked toward the boundary between the trees and the bedrock. Someone had taken a shovel and carved their initials in the dappled moss and lichen. "JKL" screamed a scar in letters five feet tall. I felt like I'd been kicked—a sucker punch to the solar plexus—and fell to my knees beside the rock's gaping wound. Frantic, I picked up dripping slabs of moss, patting them into place, covering the strange graffiti, praying the patches would grow back quickly. What sort of a hooligan would scar this gentle, comforting rock? How could anyone feel the soft embrace of this landscape and then choose to harm it? Was "JKL" some thoughtless, angry kid? Those letters didn't feel like an ill-placed declaration of love carved into a tree, but a violent assertion. I spent more than an hour trying to repair the damage, tears streaming down my face, murmuring comfort to the rock, seething at the not-quite-nameless vandal.

Hopeless, I thought as I finished my task. I can't protect even this one rocky spot that's become so special to me, can't preserve it. There's no way to keep any of it from changing. Time and the vandals of memory will have their way, too.

All I can take back from my journey are the wisps of mind and recollection, the seeds of stories, and the tears that go with them.

■ ■ ■

To endure the journey back to Boulder, I numbed myself to the pain of rending. In the Melbourne Airport, my over-stuffed duffel bag split open and Quinn found me another bag in a gift shop, one encircled with Aboriginal turtles and fish. I'd selected special gifts for my daughters and each woman friend, something to speak to her essence about one particular experience I wanted to share with her and somehow, in the confusion, my small package of carefully chosen souvenirs got lost. Some things I'd intended as gifts—a linen tea towel with two jaunty pink and gray galahs, an inexpensive reproduction of a woman's dot painting—I couldn't bear to give up.

I returned to the circle of women in Boulder and told of liquid bird calls and pictures of red desert expanses and attempts at singing harmonics; what they saw was how my experiences had changed me. They wanted the stories, the ones that opened my heart, the ones that brought tears, the ones that made me struggle for words. Some of them have been pasted to these pages, flattened like prom corsages. A few have taken shape over time, held by dreamy cobweb connec-tions. But how I've been changed? That's a question I still ask myself every day. The memories and experiences lie before me like puzzle pieces in a dream. Some fit together while others turn into mist when I reach for them. Others turn into songs that hum on the edge of hearing as I turn away.

Robin declared she just didn't have another ocean crossing within her—then sent photos and tales of more camelback treks. Dendi, the musician, one of the women of the Beechworth circle who'd played her didgeridoo as I cuddled a baby wombat, came to visit while bound for Cuba to master Latin drum rhythms. She brought me the story of Australia's "Sorry Day," when the national government officially apologized to the native people for all that they and their ancestors had suffered. Together we listened to the songs composed and performed for "Sorry Day" and cried. "Someday, we'll go together and visit the old grannies, the Koori wise women," she promised. I'm still waiting.

Sorry Day struck some ineffable chord for me, one I tried to share. "What good does it do to say you're sorry, after all those atrocities?" one friend demanded, both angry and confused. Her response made me realize that, in my struggle to convey how I'd been touched, even half the world away, by the weave of ideas and feelings that created a national day of atonement, I'd brought that story embryo out of the pouch too soon.

"It's a step, a small step, toward healing the violence, the injuries, the painful history. It doesn't fix anything—but it recognizes all the wrongs, names them—which is more than we've done," I replied, trying a bit of damage control.

"Sounds maudlin to have people dumping ashes on their heads, apologizing for things they had nothing to do with," she said.

"It wasn't like that, really," I said. "Let me play the music for you," trusting the power of rhythm and sound to reach her when my words alone could not. It helped a little.

A few years later, Jilba stopped in Boulder on a didgeridoo concert tour. "That little group of women in Beechworth has been changed by your visit," she said.

"Changed how?"

"Hard to say, exactly, but when you told the stories from your life in Boulder, about the circle of women gathering together each week for so many years, just sharing that experience started us opening up little windows into our own private worlds, sharing in different ways. I've seen things shift. It's amazing. You wouldn't think it would be so hard just to learn to love each other, would you?"

Teach me how to love you—her words echoed and swirled in my mind. Do we know how to tell one another? Can we learn?

Teach me how to love you. No grand, sweeping rules, are there? So many false starts, so many ways of saying it, often in code that has to be deciphered. Saying "I want to marry you" was once a way. Or, "I want to make love to you," or "go to bed with you," or "hold you." All those were supposed to mean love —but didn't. And just how many of those blind alleys did I wander into, anyway?

Teach me how to love you seems to expand love beyond the limits of sexual pairing. Tell me what you want, and I will listen, with respect for you and for all the experiences that make you who you are.

I wanted to tell my daughters, teach me how to love you—now, as independent young women. Let's discover what transformed mother-love can be. I come from a mother who showed her caring with dire warnings, a father who used arguments and orations. Teach me how to move beyond what distorts the rich love between us.

Teach me how to love you. It's my silent prayer to the Koori grandmothers, the tribal elders that go on living day by day.

The women's circle continued—an ongoing experiment in learning how to love each other and discovering what each of us needs to feel loved. Voicing our interests, our fears, our appreciation for each other, in the sacred space of the circle, we gradually came closer, exploring new ways to love each other.

Sometimes my Australia stories seem too romantic, even to me, but I've gradually realized that's not something negative. What are romantic stories but those that touch your heart and send your imagination spinning?

Recently I read that a stretch of the Ghan railroad reopened, snaking its way across the desert from Adelaide to Darwin in the Northern Territory, fulfilling a centuries-old dream for Australia and the isolated residents of the miniscule, remote communities along the way.

Still waiting for a conclusion, I realized that I returned with a clutch of experiences like spider eggs woven into a cocoon. And as much as my mind wants to hurry, as much as my will wants to push me forward, eggs always hatch in their own time. There is no hurrying gestation.

Quinn, Tia, and I have found ways to share more of our lives, despite the hassles of phoning across time zones and the International Date Line. When I moved to a new house in a new state, Quinn came to help me, crafting a spiral staircase to reach a closed-off tower. Tia laid shelf paper in the kitchen and spent hours patiently removing grass and weeds from an overgrown strawberry bed in my front yard. In the evening of one visit, they took over the piano in a small, local restaurant, providing an impromptu concert.

"You're Australians! Then sing us 'Waltzing Matilda,'" an enthusiastic patron said, his request close to a demand.

"People always want that song," Quinn whispered. "They think it's rousing, but when you listen to the words, it's really enormously sad. After all, it's about a sheep stealer who decides to kill himself."

"I know, it always gives me a lump in my throat," I said.

Smiling gamely, Quinn and Tia launched into a practiced "Matilda" duet that left the audience clapping for more.

Squeezing my eyes tight didn't stop my tears.

Not long ago, I encountered another writer who'd also traveled and lived down under. He, too, was changed by his encounter with the country, touched in ways that eluded words: "It's been five years and I still haven't been able to write about it," he said.

"I know, I know exactly what you mean," I replied.

ABOUT THE AUTHOR

Diana Somerville had lived in seven different states at dozens of addresses by the time she reached twenty-five, but Colorado was the one place that felt like home. So when divorce left her with a part-time job and two young daughters to support, she hunkered down in Boulder, stumbled into a career as a science writer, and began the process of transforming herself into an effective social activist, an award-winning freelance writer, editor, and teacher.

A spiritual feminist who combines real-world concerns with multifaceted idealism, she has co-taught an innovative women's studies course for non-traditional students, led political actions, and offered workshops on ritual, magic, mystery, and the mythic structure of dreams. She's the only one to have taught both women's studies and science writing at the University of Colorado.

Nearly twenty years as part of an ongoing women's spiritual circle has given her an experiential grounding in feminist theology and cosmic spirituality. Author of hundreds of magazine articles, she was a regular columnist for the *Daily Camera* in Boulder for several years before moving to Port Angeles, Washington.

After decades in semi-arid Colorado, she now lives on a bluff overlooking the Strait of Juan de Fuca and Victoria, British Columbia.

ABOUT THE COVER ARTIST

Carmel Middletent is the only Australian Aboriginal artist known to be painting in the U.S. today. Working in the powerfully symbolic Aboriginal tradition for expressing the ancient origins of life and land, she creates vivid works that have won numerous awards and been featured in solo shows on the West Coast.

"Orion" depicts a story from the archives of her mother's country, she explains: "It is said long ago in our Aboriginal mythological stories that there were blonde-haired people with blue eyes wearing dolphin pendants who would come and visit the Aboriginal people in an area in Gympie. The story also says that these people came from the star system Orion, and that they built the pyramids which can still be seen today in Gympie, where they are called the Glass House Mountains."

Born in Brisbane of Aboriginal ancestry, Carmel moved to the U.S. in 1988 and now lives in Washington state. She is writing and illustrating an autobiography, *Blue Earth, Black Shadows.* Her own experiences of personal displacement lie at the heart of her work as she continues to find new ways to reconnect with her past, keep her cultural heritage alive, and advance as an artist.

CPSIA information can be obtained
at www.ICGtesting.com
Printed in the USA
FFOW03n0753111017
40913FF

9 780977 353309